W9-CFR-941

HAS MY LAWYER CALLED YET ?

Lawrence B. Fox

Copyright ©2002 by Lawrence B. Fox

Registered with the Library of Congress

ISBN 0-9724891-0-X

Thanks to Infinity Publishing for help with this project.

All rights reserved under International and other applicable Copyright Conventions. Published in the United States of America by Lawrence B. Fox. No quotations, pictures or other portions of this book may be reproduced in any form without written permission from the author.

This book is a work of fiction. Names, characters, places and incidents are the products of the author's imagination or are used fictitiously. Any resemblance to actual events, locales or persons, living or dead, is entirely coincidental.

If you enjoy this book, you may wish to read the author's other humorous work regarding the practice of law:

There's No Justice - Just Court Costs.

Published in the United States by Fox Publications, Inc.
915 West Broad Street
Bethlehem, Pennsylvania 18018
Toll Free Telephone 1-866-4-369782   (1-866-4-FOXPUB)
Visit our website at www.lawrencebfox.com

TABLE OF CONTENTS

<u>DEDICATION</u>

To Teresa

PREFACE

This is the second book that I have written about the practice of law in a small town. Once again I have attempted to chronicle the pursuit of Justice. Justice occurs when my client wins and I get paid. Injustice occurs when my client loses and I don't get paid. There have been times when my client has lost, yet I did get paid. This is known as Sporadic Justice and arises when I've been smart enough to ask for a retainer fee.

Many of my clients start out with the misconception that Justice can be found somewhere in a courtroom. This, generally, is not the case. Courtrooms exist so that irrational people incapable of amicably resolving their differences can congregate together in an endeavor to lie simultaneously under oath at one convenient location.

Some people dislike lawyers. Yet, these are the same people who brag when a son or daughter graduates from law school. They are the same people who voluntarily enter my office believing that the Internal Revenue Code doesn't apply to them, that speed limits are for the other guy, and that their unleashed dog ought to get a free bite once in a while. I sit with a serious look on my face and take copious notes. Sooner or later I have enough material for another book.

Some of my readers have suggested that the stories I have related cannot possibly be true. Documented proof exists for review by the non-believer. As but one example, displayed after this preface, is a copy of the deed to which I have referred in Chapter 15, "The International Acquisition of Real Estate."

Chapters may be read out of sequence, since each story describes an unrelated event. The reader is encouraged to take this book along when five or 10 spare minutes might arise. Each story can be read in a relatively short period of time.

It's not possible to adequately thank the people who have made this book a reality. I stopped counting after the 15th rewrite. Cathy Rudolph typed each draft without complaint. Thanks go to Iva Ferris for her computer expertise. Dianne Pelaggi's insightful editorial comments kept me on the straight and narrow path. Encouragement from members of The Greater Lehigh Valley Writers Group proved to be invaluable.

My thanks to Harry Newman, Joseph Krycia and George Varghese, who posed with me for the cover photos. Stunned motorists driving by the day of the shoot shut down traffic for over an hour. The day after, several onlookers wrote letters to the editor, expressing concern about the return of chain gangs.

Many other people have provided expertise as necessary. As an example, the chain in the photos was purchased at the local building supply center. The knowledgeable salesman was quite helpful.

"Do you work here?"

"Yes and no. I should be over in bathroom fixtures."

"I need some chain."

"For what?"

"A chain gang."

"How many prisoners?"

"Three."

"You'll need 25 feet."

My thanks also to Robert John Penchick who took the cover photographs.

Penchick Photography: www. Penchickphoto.com.

Original copyrighted illustrations are by Dianne F. Pelaggi and Lawrence B. Fox.

Comments regarding this book are welcomed and may be sent to nfcesq@enter.net. I look forward to hearing from each one of you.

Bethlehem, Pennsylvania, September of 2002

DEED OF LAND

This indenture made this 4th day of ▮▮▮▮ ▮▮ of Our Lord One Thousand Nine Hundred and Fifty-five.

BETWEEN:

DAWSON ⊙

KLONDIKE BIG INCH LAND CO., INC.,

a body corporate duly registered for ▮▮▮▮▮ carrying on business in the Yukon Territory, having its head office for the said ▮▮▮▮▮▮ of Whitehorse, hereinafter called the "Grantor,"

OF THE FIRST PART

AND: *Larry Fo▮▮* (fill in your name) ▮▮▮ hereinafter called the "Grantee,"

OF THE SECOND PART.

WITNESSETH THAT the Grantor for good and valuable ▮▮▮▮▮▮▮▮▮ now paid by the Grantee to the Grantor (the receipt whereof is hereby by it acknowledged) doth grant, bargain, sell, alien, ▮▮▮▮▮▮▮▮▮ ▮▮▮▮▮ convey and confirm unto the Grantee, his heirs and assigns forever an estate in fee simple; ⊙ WHEREOF ▮▮

ALL AND SINGULAR that certain parcel or tract of land ▮▮▮▮▮▮▮▮ lying and being **L 425916** in the Yukon Territory more particularly known and describ▮▮ ▮▮TRACT NUMBERED

comprising by admeasurement one square inch more ▮▮▮▮▮▮ particularly described in that certain subdivision plan, prepared and acknowledged by the Grantor ▮▮▮▮▮▮▮▮ the 16th day of December, A.D. 1954 and deposited at the registered office of the Grantor in the Yuk▮▮ ▮▮▮▮▮▮▮ the whole of Lot Two hundred forty-three (243) in Group Two (2) in Yukon Territory, as said lan▮▮▮▮▮▮▮▮▮▮ of survey of record in the Legal Surveys and Aeronautical Charts Division of the Department of Mi▮▮▮▮▮ ▮▮▮▮▮ Surveys at Ottawa under number 6718, containing by admeasurement Nineteen and eleven hundr▮▮▮▮▮▮▮▮▮ more or less; together with all and singular the easements, hereditaments and appurtenances to ▮▮ ▮▮▮▮▮▮ or in any way appertaining with reversion and reversions, remainder and remainders, rents, ▮▮▮▮▮▮ ▮▮▮reof and all the estate, right, title, interest, claim, property and demand both at law and in equity ▮▮▮▮▮▮ ▮▮▮▮ of, in, to or out of the same or any part thereof;

TO HAVE AND TO HOLD the said lands and premi▮▮▮ ▮▮▮ ▮▮▮▮rtenances and every part thereof unto the said Grantee, his heirs and assigns to his and their sole use, benefit and ▮▮▮▮▮ ▮▮▮▮▮ nevertheless to the reservations, limitations, provisos and conditions expressed in the original grant thereof from the Crow▮▮

SEE OTHER SIDE

DEED OF LAND

CONTINUED

AND the Grantor for itself, its successors and assigns doth hereby covenant, promise and agree to and with the Grantee, his heirs and assigns in manner following that is to say that it shall be lawful for the Grantee, his heirs and assigns from time to time and at all times hereafter peaceably and quietly to enter into the said lands and premises and to have, hold, occupy, possess and enjoy the same without the lawful suit, hinderance, eviction, denial or disturbance of, from or by the Grantor, and also that the Grantor has a good, sure and perfect estate in fee simple in the said land and premises and good right, full po▮▮▮ and ▮▮▮ ful▮ thereof, lawful authority to sell and convey the same in manner and form as they are hereby sold and conveyed and mentioned or ▮▮plied, ▮▮ to be and the same are free from encumbrances, subject ▮▮▮▮▮▮ to the provisions herein contained;

AND this conveyance and everything herein ▮▮▮▮▮▮ shall be wholly subject to a perpetual easement for in▮▮▮▮▮ egress, to, from, over and upon the tract herein conveyed ▮▮▮ use of the owner or owners of all other tracts of land and ▮▮▮▮ seen herein described and further described and set forth ▮▮ ▮▮▮ subdivision plan hereinabove mentioned and without restr▮▮▮▮▮▮ generality of the foregoing clause the same shall not in a▮▮▮▮▮▮▮▮ construed as a derogation from the grant hereby effected ▮▮▮▮ Grantee herein, and the Grantor hereby grants unto the ▮▮▮▮▮▮ perpetual easement for ingress and egress, to, from, over ▮▮▮ ▮▮▮▮ any or all of the tracts of land or parcels of land in the subdivi▮▮▮▮▮▮ aforesaid as may from time to time remain vested in the ▮▮▮▮▮▮▮

AND the Grantor covenants with the Grantee that ▮▮ ▮▮▮▮ done no act to encumber the said lands;

AND the Grantor releases to the Grantee all its ▮▮▮▮▮▮▮▮ upon the said lands;

The provisions of the Land Titles Act being Ch. 162 of the Revised Statutes of Canada, 1952 and amendments thereto shall not apply to this Deed of Conveyance and in addition but not so as to limit the generality of the foregoing the Grantor shall not be obliged to do any acts or execute any instruments as may be necessary to better secure the title of the Grantee or to provide a transfer to the within described lands and premises registerable under the aforesaid Act nor to deliver or have registered a subdivision plan of the aforementioned Lot 243 or any portion thereof;

Wherever the singular or masculine are used throughout this indenture the same shall be construed as meaning the plural or the feminine or body corporate or politic where the context or the parties hereto so require;

IN WITNESS WHEREOF the corporate seal of the ▮▮▮ has been hereunto affixed in the presence of its proper ▮▮▮ duly authorized in that behalf;

▮▮▮porate seal of **KLONDIKE BIG INCH LAND CO., INC.** was hereunto affixed in the presence of:

John E. Bak▮▮ jr.
PRESIDENT

Joseph B. H▮▮▮▮
SECRETARY-TREASURER

PRINTED IN U.S.A.

CHAPTER ONE:
A LEG UP

Ronald Muncy was a part-time crook and a full-time liar. Nearly every member of the Northampton County public defender's staff had represented him regarding one criminal charge or another. Muncy didn't possess the ingenuity or imagination to engage in any significant felonious undertakings. Rather, he would try to pass a worthless check, or attempt to shoplift an $8 item. He always got caught, as if that result were part of his plan. He always steadfastly maintained his innocence. There was always a time-consuming jury trial.

Tommy Hines worked at the courthouse. He was 20 years old and labored as a clerk in the Prothonotary's Office. At night, he attended classes at the community college. He hoped someday to receive his bachelor's degree in marketing. Until then, he would have to live at home with his parents.

Loretta Figlear was employed at the courthouse, too, in the Recorder of Deeds Office. She had unblemished alabaster skin, perfect teeth, and at 19 years of age, a smile that the Mona Lisa would have envied. She and Tommy took part in early morning county-sponsored yoga classes, and soon began to eat lunch at the same cafeteria table. Then they fell in love.

Courtroom No. 1 was built to be impressive, and its oversized features commanded reverence and respect from those who dared enter. The spectator pews boasted seating for 400. The walls stretched 60 feet upward, supporting an ornate ceiling half the size of a football field, embossed with a hand-painted stenciled pattern encircling a 20-foot hanging chandelier. Thirty-foot high windows along the side walls were accentuated with polished mahogany interior shutters that worked as efficiently as the day they were installed in the 1860s, about the time of our nation's Civil War. This ornate chamber was now the domain of Northampton County's President Judge, The Honorable Clinton Budd Palmer.

The courthouse was built a century before the advent of air conditioning. An alcove large enough to hangar a four-engine jet airplane existed above Courtroom No. 1. It was designed to dissipate naturally the summer's hot air through vented duct work. A small door hidden from public view in the third floor archives led to the alcove. One day, while he was dropping off some old files, Tommy discovered the forgotten door and the unoccupied alcove.

"Holy Hannah!" he thought to himself.

He immediately shared his findings with Loretta during lunch.

"It sounds creepy," she said.

"No, Loretta, it's quiet - it's ... secluded," her lover insisted. "We could be ... alone ... "

The mammoth courthouse was busy that day. Over in Courtroom No. 4, some union organizers were seeking an injunction. Courtroom No. 5 was the setting for a guardianship petition. And in Courtroom No. 1, Ronald Muncy's fifth trial in six years was about to get underway. This time, he was charged with breaking into a vending machine. I had been assigned to represent him. I didn't like my client - not because I thought he was guilty. Rather, he was testing the judicial system when no test was warranted. He should have taken his punishment like a man. I suggested as much to him under my breath as we picked a jury.

"I didn't do nothin' wrong," he protested. "There was hundreds of fingerprints on that vending machine besides mine."

True. But only his prints were found on the interior

coin box. That subtle point of evidence seemed to escape Mr. Muncy.

"I'm innocent," he reiterated.

The jury was empaneled by early afternoon. By 3 p.m., the assistant district attorney had presented his entire case, including a fingerprint expert. In a flash of brilliance, my client decided to take the witness stand in his own defense.

- - - - - - - - - - - - - - - - - - - -

An injunction had just been denied in Courtroom No. 4. A guardian had been appointed in Courtroom No. 5. And at the Prothonotary's Office, Tommy was taking his 15-minute afternoon break. He walked briskly to the Recorder of Deeds Office, where the unsuspecting Loretta enjoyed a simultaneous recess.

"Wait 'til you see this big attic, Loretta! Architecturally speaking, there's nothing like it - not even the Sistine Chapel!"

Loretta knew that on her salary, an excursion to the Vatican was not imminent. If Tommy possessed an interest in 19th century construction, perhaps she ought to expend the effort to share in his enthusiasm. There was one minor concern.

"Are there any spiders up there, Tommy?"

"Spiders? No ... no spiders. None whatsoever," Tommy assured his trusting companion. "The door has been shut for years, so they haven't had a way to get in."

- - - - - - - - - - - - - - - - - - - -

"Do you swear to tell the Truth, and nothing but the Truth, so as you shall answer to God on The Last Great Day?"

Muncy looked into the piercing eyes of the bailiff, and responded with an unhesitating *"Yes."* The jury was about to hear his side of the story. Judge Palmer and I looked at each other, both silently wincing in pain.

Tommy cautiously opened the forgotten interior archive door. Loretta tentatively peeked in.

"Where are the lights?" she asked.

"Aren't any. Isn't that cool?"

The couple entered, and sat down on a 12-inch wooden floor joist cut nearly two centuries ago from virgin Pennsylvania forest. Tommy gazed lovingly at the object of his desire.

"I think I hear a spider," Loretta noted.

Tommy smiled knowingly and offered a comforting kiss.

I stood up, and began the unrehearsed inquiry of my client. "Mr. Muncy, please tell the jury your side of the story."

"Well, you see it was like this - I didn't break into no vending machine. I swear it. I had more than enough money that day to buy the candy bar."

The picture was starting to come into focus for Loretta. "Tommy," she said, "I'm not sure this is a good idea. What if someone ... ya know ... sees us?"

"That could *never* happen up here," the lovesick Tommy assured the hesitating Loretta, who continued to experience difficulty dedicating all of her attention to the task at hand.

"No one's been in this place for years."

"I just felt a gigantic spider touch my - "

"It's just me," the reassuring Tommy clarified.

"Huh? Oh. Right. Well, O.K.," Loretta said.

"But then the dang vending machine jammed," Muncy explained to the jury, "so I took out the 8-inch screw driver I always carry, so I could ... er ... fix the problem. I didn't mean to do nothin' criminal - on my mother's grave."

- - - - - - - - - - - - - - - - - - - -

"Tommy, I ... I can't keep my balance on this rafter. Wouldn't this be ... um ... easier in your car?"

"Our break is over in five minutes. I love you, Loretta."

- - - - - - - - - - - - - - - - - - - -

Muncy decided it was time for some drama. He stood up in the witness box and faced the jury - all 24 eyes. He raised his right index finger straight into the air.

"If I'm lying, may God strike me dead with a bolt of-"

- - - - - - - - - - - - - - - - - - - -

A spider decided to spin in for a closer view of the entangled lovers. It landed on Loretta's nose. She screamed, kicked Tommy, then rolled off the rafter. Her left leg popped through the plaster floorboard of the ancient alcove, traveling downward until her dainty hips ended her unscheduled descent. Her naked leg now projected from the ceiling of Courtroom No. 1, directly above the witness box.

The breach of the ceiling by Loretta's shapely leg had dislodged a section of heavy plaster, which fell to earth, hitting Muncy squarely on the head. To the astonishment of the courtroom's spectators, he lost consciousness and slumped to the floor. When he came to, he brushed the plaster dust from his hair and shoulders. Then he turned to the judge.

"I'm guilty. As a matter of fact, I've never been innocent. NEVER," he blubbered. "I'm bad, but I'm going straight. I ain't never gonna do nothin' wrong never again," he confessed with heart-felt candor.

My client's frankness impressed me. But I wasn't

sure if the jury had heard this important recantation. Twenty-four eyes still focused upward at the suspended naked leg flailing about. Judge Palmer took back control of his courtroom. He banged his gavel.

"Ladies and gentlemen of the jury. Please. It's just a leg. We've all seen one before. Kindly turn your attention to the case at leg ... I mean at HAND!"

Tommy finally pulled Loretta to safety. She took the rest of the day off, and later called Tommy at his parents' house to break off their romance.

As for Ronald Muncy, he was found guilty. He thanked me anyway for doing a satisfactory job, and called again six months later to inform me that he had just been awarded a high school equivalency diploma, and that he ultimately planned to attend law school.

"With all my courtroom experience, I'll probably be able to get credit for the first year of classes," he explained.

CHAPTER TWO:
THE LOST FILE

A magical feeling envelops me whenever I visit Crystal Cave near Kutztown, or Lost Cave in Hellertown. Eastern Pennsylvania is blessed with such natural wonders because of its subterranean limestone deposits. Over time spanning millions of years, underground aquifers and rivers have dissolved the limestone, and have carved out these magnificent hidden crystalline chambers.

Countless patient stalagmites rise silently from the floor. The dripping stalactites reach down from the ceiling, growing, albeit microscopically, in an ageless endeavor to touch their stalagmite friends. Centimeters of growth are measured in millennia.

The tour guide leads our clustered group of shivering amateur spelunkers along a forgotten underground stream. It's July, but we can see each other's breath in the cool air. The cave walls glisten with moisture as the guide directs her flashlight onto an ancient geological formation.

"And here we see the end product of millions of years of deposits derived from percolating calcareous water."

She is a senior at Pennsylvania State University, and hopes to become a mining engineer. During this, her last summer before graduation, the cave serves as both her home away from home, and her source of income.

If only every state had subterranean limestone and percolating calcareous waters so that there would be even more wondrous caves to visit!

- -

It was an unfortunate scenario upon which I had all too often been consulted - the eviction of an indigent tenant. But Rachel DeFazio's plight was more critical than most. She was the single mother of a 2-year-old, and she was six months pregnant. The father had disappeared, taking with him their meager savings of $200. Her corporate landlord's absentee representative had just served her with a final notice of eviction. The landlord, with a California business address, planned to throw my newest client and her toddler into the street next week. I hardly had enough tissues to get her through our meeting. I wanted to help, but I wasn't sure how. She had, unfortunately, ignored all her rights to appeal the eviction process.

"I didn't know nothin' 'bout no appeal," she whimpered as she applied another tissue to her eye. "I've been busy takin' care of my kid. How was I supposed to know my boyfriend wasn't payin' the rent on time?"

Her pleas for help, issued between sobs, had touched my soul, for it appeared there was no one else left, save her obstetrician, to assist her.

The eviction notice bore a convenient 800 number for assistance.

"I'll place a call in the morning," I promised the tear-stained Rachel. "I'll let you know what I find out."

"Sunshine Realty Association" was located in Southern California. The automated voice mail advised me that with more than 4,000 apartments to maintain across the country, Sunshine Realty was one of the largest rental firms in the nation. The message ended abruptly with an address where the listener could obtain rates for one, two and three bedroom apartments.

I contacted the Clerk of Courts at the courthouse, gave her the term number of the DeFazio eviction notice, and asked if any attorney had entered an appearance in this litigation.

"Yes," she confirmed. "The Law Firm of Singletary,

Shipsworth, and Farmer."

The Lehigh Valley is not large. There are only 30 or 40 law firms operating in the area, and every lawyer in the bar association is aware of each other's existence and reputation. Some firms have been around for more than a hundred years. I had never heard of Singletary, Shipsworth, and Farmer.

"S.S.& F." as its web page began, was a 350-person firm, maintaining its principal office in Philadelphia, with branch offices in New York, Chicago, and Los Angeles. Last month, it created a satellite office in the Lehigh Valley, and so 20 lawyers were relocated overnight to our back-woods community. They took over the top two floors of the Edison Building in downtown Easton. When the branch office opened for business, it became, with the turn of a key, the single largest law firm in the valley.

I decided to call S.S.&F., to get the name of the specific attorney who had been assigned to handle the DeFazio eviction case. A polite secretary answered.

"Singletary, Shipsworth, & Farmer ... may I help you?" Her British accent snapped with sophistication and importance. It was best not to waste her time.

"Could you please tell me which attorney handles evictions for Sunshine Realty?"

"One moment, please ... "

The second movement of Brahms' Third Piano Concerto filled my telephone receiver. The British receptionist returned.

"Does your inquiry concern an industrial, corporate, business, or personal eviction?"

Suddenly I was transported back to my first workers' compensation case involving United Delivery Service. My client had injured his knee while climbing out from one of its delivery trucks. I contacted the law firm representing the company, and advised the receptionist of the type of case I was handling.

"I am sorry," she replied. "The lawyers who deal

- 9 -

with knees are at a knee seminar all week. The only lawyers present in the office today work solely with ankles and hips."

Had law really become this specialized?

"Well, what type of eviction is it?" my British friend repeated.

"Your firm is evicting a single mother. Rachel DeFazio."

"One moment, please."

Brahms had begun his third movement. The receptionist returned in the middle of a crescendo.

"Attorney Gregory VanOutten handles evictions of individuals. Would you like me to transfer you?"

"Yes." Brahms reappeared, momentarily, and then vanished.

"Mr. VanOutten's office. Claudia speaking."

I introduced myself and described Ms. DeFazio's predicament. I inquired if Attorney VanOutten might be willing to consider some form of mutually beneficial resolution of this unfortunate matter. Claudia seemed put off.

"One moment, please," she huffed.

Brahms soon ventured into his fourth movement.

"Sir, I've located the file. It appears your client failed to perfect a timely appeal. I'm afraid there is nothing more we can do. The eviction will proceed as scheduled."

"I appreciate your candor," I said. "But quite frankly, I was hoping to speak with Attorney VanOutten himself in an endeavor to convince him to extend compassion toward a single mother who is preg - "

"Excuse me, sir," Claudia interrupted. "Mr. VanOutten doesn't talk to anyone about evictions. Such minor matters are left to his paralegal, Mr. Finkelbone."

Unfortunately, Finkelbone was out to lunch. No one knew when he might return and DeFazio was to be evicted by the sheriff's constable in less than 72 hours. I theorized that if I could personally meet with the landlord's representative, surely the milk of human compassion would flow, and I would, at the very least, achieve a temporary stay of eviction. Against her better judgment, good Claudia gave me an appointment for the next morning with the elusive Finkelbone.

The Edison Building in downtown Easton hadn't really changed during the past 40 years. The same could be said about downtown Easton. A bank took up the entire first floor of the Edison's eight stories. The second through sixth floors were filled with the usual nondescript insurance offices, dentists, realtors, and stockbrokers. The tired, architecturally unimaginative building struggled with a less than 70 percent occupancy rate, and so Singletary, Shipsworth & Farmer had little difficulty taking over both the seventh and eighth floors.

I hadn't had occasion to visit the Edison for more than two years. The last time was to track down some short-lived home improvement "professional" on the third floor who had no known home address. The 1920's style floor tile still adorned the lobby; the street-level windows had the same rounded arches; and the elevators still rattled as carved bronze arrows swept left or right, indicating the level upon which each car stopped. I escaped mutilation in the revolving lobby door, and took the left elevator up to the seventh floor.

The old cables strained as the rickety elevator labored slowly to lift me to my destination.

"What a dump," I thought. My temporary prison came to an unsteady halt, signaling the ancient elevator door to open. I expected to step into a poorly lit hallway smelling of janitorial cleanser. I was mistaken.

My very first step off the elevator landed me in thick, luxurious aqua-blue carpet. Had I dropped my pen, or some false teeth, or my case file into its depths, such articles would have disappeared forever. Paintings by the Dutch masters adorned the imposing coffered paneled walls. Mozart's Jupiter Symphony floated in the air. Cut crystal chandeliers defused the cascading light onto hand-carved ceiling tiles. The receptionist appeared half a basketball court's distance away, seated at a desk inlaid with mother-of-pearl. If any client ever dared ask what these lawyers charged, he likely couldn't afford the fee.

"May I help you?" It was the Brit.

My client didn't possess the $285 necessary to pay her monthly rent. She did not have any money to pay me. I was now schlepping through a carpet that cost in excess of $80,000. Yes, the receptionist could help me - help me find the nearest exit so I wouldn't make an ass of myself.

"I'm here to see Mr. Finkelbone," I whispered.

"Won't you have a seat?"

A seat? How about that French provincial number resting next to the Ming Dynasty vase. I could sell both and send DeFazio's two kids to college. I cautiously lowered my derriere onto the very edge of the museum-quality 17th century mahogany heirloom.

A gentleman approached from stage left. He was Finkelbone from head to toe. He extended a limp, disinterested hand.

"I'm Ralph Finkelbone," he announced.

"I know," I confirmed. I followed him into a conference room, lifting my feet as high as possible.

The conference room was more plush than the waiting room. Alabaster ashtrays accentuated a gold leaf embossed table designed and built by Stradivarius. Portraits of the 20 attorneys serving the office lined the walls, each positioned exactly seven inches apart. Not a single face smiled. All wore white button-down shirts and hand-tailored suits, including the women. A 6-foot Greek sculpture of Zeus composed entirely of white marble stood at the corner of the room, surrounded by fresh orchids. It was here that we would discuss DeFazio's $285 rental issue.

Tanned Finkelbone sat across from me, his distant eyes glazed over, his mind elsewhere. Not a wrinkle sullied his $2,000 imported Italian suit. The reflections from his diamond stickpin nestled within his silk tie blinded me in the light of the crystal chandelier.

I explained DeFazio's plight.

"Counselor," he yawned with all the sparkle of a guest speaker at a mortician's convention, "Singletary, Shipsworth, & Farmer maintains an ethical duty to its client, the landlord, to reclaim the leasehold premises. Your client has not paid the rent. All appeals have lapsed."

"She's six months pregnant and has a 2-year-old child!"

"That is regrettable, but legally irrelevant," came the detached response.

"You leave me no choice. I will appear before the court 24 hours before the constable seeks to perform his eviction. I will obtain emergency relief!"

It was a hollow threat and Finkelbone knew it.

"As you wish," the human manikin mumbled. "We'll send one of our associates."

I was suddenly the captain of the luxury liner, Titanic, feeling the subdued, yet unmistakable impact of the iceberg as it ripped through the hull of his luckless ship.

"Will there be anything else?" Finkelbone asked.

I had overstayed my welcome. That's when I heard it, or perhaps I just felt it. A tremble? A movement? An iceberg? I glanced up and noted that the unsmiling portrait of one of the 20 lawyers - the photograph nearest the picture window - was now tilted off-center. Had there been an earthquake? Finkelbone said nothing, noticed nothing. He had been in a self-induced trance since our useless meeting began.

"Will there be anything else?" he repeated.

I took my leave of the crystal palace and reentered the mundane lobby six floors below. The scene as I exited the elevator was not as lifeless as when I had arrived. The unexpected reverberation of the building had not gone unnoticed by the other tenants. Forty or 50 animated souls had emerged from the bank. Several were pointing toward a large crack in the dome ceiling. Some swore out loud that the chasm was growing larger by the minute. I had even, unwittingly, stepped on pieces of fallen plaster.

I proceeded to the revolving exterior door, but

strangely, it would not budge, so I left by way of a side door and headed back to the office.

The next morning I grabbed the daily paper on the way into the office - the office I had furnished in "early poverty" style 29 years earlier for less than $300. The lead article on page one quickly caught my eye: *Sinkhole Swallowing Edison - Downtown Easton Sealed Off.*

The article quoted the city street department foreman at length. A self-appointed sinkhole expert, he now laid claim to this, his fleeting chance at fame.

"You see, this whole area, no pun intended, is composed of limestone. Subterranean percolating calcareous waters infiltrate the limestone, sometimes by an unseen diversion of the course of an aquifer. Caverns can form that ultimately produce a sinkhole visible at the surface level. Or maybe it was just a broken water main. Or an over-active gopher. We're checking all possibilities."

By mid-afternoon the hole, which had initially appeared at the southwest corner of the building, had grown to a diameter of 30 feet, and was now eating away at the foundation. The structure appeared to be leaning ever so slightly to the east.

His Honor, the Mayor, decided to take control. He issued an executive edict mandating that no one could enter the stricken building until the actual degree of damage could be assessed.

By nightfall, the mortally wounded building had tilted three inches more. Police taped and barricaded two city blocks. The hole was now 60 feet across. Gushing water could be heard far below. A large crowd stood witness to the unfolding events. Conversation was lively and speculative.

"Once that building falls into the hole, maybe they will discover a new cave," some blue-haired old lady told her excited friend. "That would be a boon for the downtown tourist business!"

Others weren't quite as upbeat about the unexpected phenomenon. The lawyers employed at Singletary,

Shipsworth & Farmer who had, until yesterday, been tenants on the seventh and eighth floors of what was now being referred to as the *Leaning Tower of Easta* wanted to temporarily reenter The Edison to remove their most important personal property and files. One of the attorneys, Mr. VanOutten, requested and received an emergency audience with His Honor, the Mayor. VanOutten sought permission to access the structure before it was too late.

"Nothin' doin'," His Honor reiterated. "I'm directly responsible for public safety. You could die in there!"

And then a miracle occurred. A Mr. Herbert Ledbetter contacted the Philadelphia Office of Singletary, Shipsworth & Farmer, to advise that his internationally recognized company, Treasure Savers Ltd. specialized in extricating personal property from condemned and stricken buildings. There was no time to lose. The law firm drafted an emergency petition for special relief and submitted it to the court, seeking to temporarily nullify the mayor's order precluding entry into the building.

The judge granted the lawyers a five-hour reprieve. Commencing at 2 p.m., and ending at 7 p.m. sharp, the professional daredevils employed by Treasure Savers would be permitted to enter the Edison Building to remove personal property from the seventh and eighth floors.

Time was running out. The stricken edifice had now sunk more than two feet into the ground and it was leaning almost a foot to the east. Intermittent cracking and snapping noises could be heard coming from the uninhabited bowels of the building.

The fearless spelunkers from Treasure Savers donned their fire-resistant suits with attached air hoses and radio antennae, and entered the doomed structure. Others from their team positioned several 18-wheeled moving vans near the police barricades, ready to accept the goods as they were removed. Each time a team member emerged with a priceless painting, delicate piece of furniture, office files, or combination safe, the admiring crowd would issue forth a collective cheer of encouragement. Perspiration streamed down the heroes' faces, for there was neither electrical power nor air conditioning to service the building. Everything had to be lugged down seven or eight flights of stairs.

After five hours of tireless effort, almost everything of value had been removed from the law offices and had been secured within the waiting moving trucks. As nightfall approached, the police again cordoned off the building. Treasure Savers moved the trucks to a safe location. Ten days later, the entire building disappeared into the ever-widening sinkhole. The old lady with the blue hair was right. Never had so many people come to visit downtown Easton.

Treasure Savers was appropriately named. The company had succeeded in securing everything of value. Without such heroics, each priceless possession, every irreplaceable file, would surely have been lost. S.S.&F.'s Lehigh Valley satellite office would again be able to serve its discriminating clientele. VanOutten made arrangements to relocate the offices to an unimaginative corporate complex in the township industrial park where he was assured no sinkhole had ever appeared. He signed a 10-year lease that required monthly rent in excess of the annual gross national product of Luxembourg.

"I want our stuff moved in by next Thursday," he instructed his trusted paralegal, Finkelbone.

"Precisely," Ralph mumbled.

Easier said than done. Finkelbone tried to locate Treasure Savers in the telephone book, on the world-wide-web, via the chamber of commerce, and ultimately through The Globernoski Detective Agency.

"Not that scam again," Detective Globernoski sighed.

"I beg your pardon," Finkelbone repeated from the cellphone in his leased Jaguar.

"Them guys are con-artists. They surface when there's a potential disaster, grab people's property under the pretext that they will safely protect it, and then they disappear without a trace."

This information was not well received by

VanOutten.

"When you negotiated with Treasure Savers, didn't you request any references?" VanOutten inquired of pale Finkelbone.

"Well, you see, sir, there wasn't that much time. The building had begun to tip - "

"Did you have them sign a bond? Did you obtain adequate insurance coverage?"

"I - "

"You realize, Finklebone, that our property was only insured for loss if it was located in the building. When we agreed to have it removed, our standard coverage lapsed, and Treasure Savers' coverage, assuming they had any, took over, since the goods were then in their control."

"That may present a problem, since they appear to have been thieves," Finkelbone reasoned.

Treasure Savers was never seen nor heard from again. The same could be said about the marble statue of Zeus, the priceless furniture, all the files, and Finkelbone who chose early retirement, and was rumored to have taken a position as a doorman at a hotel in West Virginia.

VanOutten and S.S.&F. experienced some awkward moments as well. Without any furniture or files, and no insurance coverage, transition to the new leasehold in the industrial park was delayed. The burdensome rent, however, remained due each month, a concept with which Rachel DeFazio could certainly have lent a sympathetic ear.

Her eviction hearing was continued indefinitely until her file could be located. Until then, she chose to live in her apartment.

CHAPTER THREE:
GOLDEN DRAGON - GREEN LOTUS

Those of us growing up in the 1950s in Bethlehem, Pennsylvania, were forced to endure a decade of gastrointestinal deprivation. These were the days of slow food. Pre-McDonalds dark ages. Colonel Sanders was just a Second Lieutenant and had not yet developed his secret recipe for extra-crispy chicken. There were no Wendy's, Burger Kings, or Taco Bells. Subway was something located exclusively underground in New York City.

The only Chinese restaurant within 30 miles was situated across the Delaware River in a different world - Phillipsburg, New Jersey. Phillipsburg is a strange place. No resident calls the town by its given name. It's *P-burg* (pronounced *Pea-burg*).

P-burgians find their name-altering behavior unremarkable. Outsiders instinctively conform to the pronunciation if they wish to survive in this alien world. Waitresses in P-burg ask if customers would like a glass of *wudder* with their meals. And at the service station, if one buys $12 of gasoline and pays with a $20 bill, the gas station attendant will hand back money and say, "Ate your change!"

My family went to P-burg in the 1950s solely for the Chinese food, after which we would quickly flee back home across the Delaware. More recently, the Delaware River Bridge Authority began requiring a 50 cent toll from those leaving New Jersey entering Pennsylvania. The opposite is not mandated. As the old adage goes: It costs nothing to enter New Jersey. Only to get out.

This childhood experience fostered a life-long love of good Asian food. Today, I don't have to travel to planet P-burg. Chinese food eateries are everywhere. The House of the Golden Dragon on 14th Street in Bethlehem opened three years ago, and serves exquisite chow fun. The scene inside is always the same. Clanging pots. Rising steam. Cups of food being tossed into the air. An overworked slender Asian man and his wife labor over shooting flames to keep pace with the lunch-time crowd.

My attention, however, is always drawn to the third worker.

"Your order is number 56," she says to the customer ahead of me. "Ready in 10 minutes. Your change is $2.84."

She is nine years old, and child labor laws seem not to apply to her. While her classmates study dance, this fourth grader is running a restaurant.

"May I help you?" she inquires with black piercing eyes, as she smiles at me. She always smiles. She appears to enjoy her work. When I was nine, I was irritated if asked to clean my room. For a moment, I stood transfixed as I studied the features of this bilingual 60-pound dynamo.

"May I help you, sir?" she asked again. I came to my senses.

"Yes. The chow fun. I would like a pint of chicken chow fun."

She turned to the cooks, whom I assume were her mother and father. "E pinne zee chow fun," she called out in unhesitating Chinese. One of the cooks nodded and threw some food in the air.

"You want anything else?"

"No MSG."

"OK."

She turned back to the cooks. "Bo yo whey ching."

One of the cooks nodded and threw more food in the air.

My young hostess used an abacus to calculate the sum due, including the applicable Pennsylvania sales tax. She took my payment, stretched on tip-toes to peer into the cash drawer, and immediately tendered the correct change.

I've tried to chat with her parents on occasion. But these people are workers, not conversationalists. And it's uncomfortable because the daughter must serve as their interpreter. Usually, any verbal exchange is cut short by the ringing of the phone - for it's the child restaurateur who must reach for the receiver.

"Golden Dragon. May I help you?"

- - - - - - - - - - - - - - - - - - - -

Long before the Golden Dragon took up residence on 14th Street, I became involved in municipal law. The practice of municipal law is unique. Typically, the solicitor advises elected officials how to comply with the law, while the officials seek to achieve political goals in an ethical and cost-effective manner.

I remember my first case representing Wynslow Township. The health and code inspector had cited Dan DeLeone for the alleged violation of Township ordinance R-45-37: permitting weeds in excess of two feet in height to exist upon private property located within a non-agricultural zone. DeLeone ignored the code inspector's certified letter demanding that he cease and desist from such illegal conduct. The weeds, monopolizing the better part of an acre, soon grew to nearly three feet in height.

"Can't you do something?" Township Commissioner Hassler pressed me during an informal workshop. "I've received over 20 complaints about them stinkin' weeds this month alone from voters in my district."

"I'll get right on it, Commissioner," I assured him.

I filed a formal complaint before the local magistrate, accusing DeLeone of permitting weeds to flourish, said conduct constituting a summary violation of Township ordinance R-45-37. The magistrate scheduled a hearing for the 24th of the month.

On the designated date, I appeared before the magistrate in the company of my star witness, the code enforcement officer, Moses Thistledown. DeLeone showed up, too, without witnesses or legal counsel. The magistrate called the proceedings to order. I had initiated the charges, so I possessed the burden of proof. I called my first and only witness, Thistledown.

"Now, Mr. Thistledown, what is growing on Mr. DeLeone's property?" I began.

"Objection, Your Honor," DeLeone called out as he rose to his feet. "First, learned counsel got to prove I own the land in question; then he got to show this here witness is an expert in botany who can distinguish between fauna, flora, and weeds. No foundation has been laid yet."

My goose was cooked. DeLeone had been watching his share of prime time TV. He was right. I should have brought certified records confirming he owned the offending real estate. And Thistledown was no weedologist. From that moment on I swore I'd never again be unprepared in a township or municipal proceeding.

As the years passed in Wynslow Township, Chinese restaurants began springing up everywhere. The Green Lotus at the new mall soon developed a sizable luncheon trade. The other six Chinese restaurants in the Township were also flourishing, but there was one difference between them and the Green Lotus. Taxes. I remember when I received the call from the Township's independent auditor, CPA Bill Windfall.

"Larry, I just finished my review of the business privilege taxes due at the new mall. Each of the 35 tenants has filed the required accounting for last year, with one exception - The Green Lotus. They didn't send in a dime. I think the township is probably owed anywhere between $1,300 and $2,000. The commissioners want you to collect it."

Ever since my overgrown weed investigation days, I had learned to do my homework before filing formal legal papers. So initially, it was important to determine who actually was responsible for payment of the tax. Was the Green Lotus a corporation, a partnership, or sole proprietorship? Was I dealing with a fictitious name, and had the name been duly registered?

I wrote a certified letter to the restaurant, requesting that its owner tender an accounting of gross sales for the previous year, and accompany the report with a check for the corresponding business privilege tax due. My letter was unclaimed and three weeks later was returned to my office. It was time for the direct approach.

It was noon on Saturday. I drove over to the Green Lotus for lunch. The narrow and cramped quarters boasted just three aluminum chairs with red plastic seats. I saw no other furniture. This was a take-out only facility. The menu taped to the door confirmed that chicken chow fun, and scores of other delicacies, awaited me inside. I joined seven or eight other hungry customers, all of whom now stood at the front counter facing the cramped open-view kitchen. Again, a slender man and woman, each in their mid-30s were tossing food in the air. They stood before open flames, steam rising from a gas stove crowded with large metal woks. They worked in concert, passing each other as they over-filled little paper containers with food. And again, it was the third participant who caught my attention. This one might have been eight years old. She alone maintained contact with the customers, addressed them in chronological order, and periodically would call out an order in Chinese while one cook or the other would nod a response.

"May I help you?" she asked as I moved up to the counter behind which she sat.

"A pint of chicken chow fun without any MSG, please."

"No monosodium glutamate?"

A bilingual chemist, too.

"Correct," I confirmed.

"Bin chow fun gee may. Na sam poo." One of the cooks nodded, and threw a handful of white noodles into the air.

"Are those your parents?" I asked.

"Yes. Your number is 16. Ready in 10 minutes."

She discussed food, not family.

"Might I talk to them when they are not so busy?"

"They don't speak English. That is $4.85, please."

This hard-working family had no time to spare. I took my tasty chow fun home, and returned to the mall at three o'clock. The Green Lotus was, for the moment, devoid of customers. The father sliced piles of onions. The mother prepared noodles. The eight-year-old stuffed won ton shells. The smell of hundreds of recently prepared lunches hung in the air. I approached the daughter.

"I'm Larry Fox. I am an attorney for the Township of Wynslow."

The daughter appeared neither impressed nor concerned. She called to her parents. They approached. As I spoke, the young girl interpreted.

"A letter I sent three weeks ago was never claimed."

The daughter advised her parents, who responded in Chinese. She then relayed their answer.

"All mail is forwarded to New York City. We don't read it."

"The township may be owed taxes. Who owns this restaurant?"

The parents shrugged their shoulders - an unspoken but internationally recognized gesture. The father again mentioned New York City.

The next day, I sent a letter to the mall business office. I asked who presently owned the Green Lotus Restaurant, who on behalf of the tenant had initially executed the lease, and how rent was paid. I asked for a copy of the current lease. The mall office responded quickly. The lease was inarticulately drafted and failed to identify the Green Lotus as a corporation, partnership, or individual proprietorship. Someone using formal Chinese block characters had signed the document. The mall cover letter advised that rent was received on time each month from New York by an untitled check signed in the same type of Chinese characters. It wasn't clear who or what the tenant was. But the rent checks showed up promptly, and never bounced. Someone maintaining a business address on the 38th floor of the Empire State Building had initially executed the contract.

Next was the Pennsylvania Corporation Bureau. It had no registration or information under the name of "Green Lotus." Ten days and four letters later, I still had no idea who owned this take-out eatery.

Back at the municipal office, I poured over the health and food inspection certificates. Someone must have paid for the annual health and food sales permits. I uncovered an untitled check signed in Chinese block characters. It, too, was sent from New York.

The township commissioners were not inclined to set a precedent regarding non-payment of taxes. I was instructed to continue my research and find the owner of the restaurant. I was to collect from this mysterious person or entity the business privilege tax due. Period.

I wrote a certified letter to the representative of the Green Lotus, 38th Floor, Empire State Building, New York City. The letter was returned unopened within a week.

That was it. No more games. I retained a detective agency in New York. Lee Gumm was assigned to the case. He took an elevator ride to the 38th floor and discovered a one-room office staffed by a lone receptionist wearing a red wig. She knew nothing about the Green Lotus. She did admit that on Monday mornings at 10 o'clock, an Asian man dropped off a bundle of about 500 checks signed in Chinese block characters. Her job was to mail each check to designated addresses on an accompanying computer print-out. She also faxed all written phone messages to a number in New York's Chinatown. She had no idea who she worked for, but the pay and the view were good. She had been there four years.

It was Lee Gumm on the phone. Suddenly I was transformed into Humphrey Bogart as we searched for the Maltese Falcon.

"This is Gumm. On Monday, I shadowed the Asian guy to Chinatown. I think you and I need to meet face-to-face."

"Just tell me who owns the Green Lotus and I'll send him a bill for the tax - "

"We need to talk face-to-face," he repeated flatly.

"Well, O.K.," I agreed. "I'm about 60 miles from Manhattan. Can we meet somewhere about half way?"

"Sure. How about P-burg," Gumm offered. "There's a Chinese restaurant there, called - "

"The House of Wah?"

"Yeah! The House of Wah! How did you know?"

"Went there as a kid," I responded.

"How about 2 p.m. tomorrow?"

"Two. O.K." I kept my sentences short and simple - just like Bogie. But then I started thinking like a lawyer. I had never met Gumm.

"How will I know who you are?"

"Don't worry. I'll know who you are."

Damn. I wish I had said that. Bogie would have said that.

- - - - - - - - - - - - - - - - - - -

The House of Wah was just as I remembered it. Strings of glass beads cascaded in front of the entrance door. There were dragon ashtrays, low wattage hanging lights enclosed in silken baskets, and mysterious Chinese music. I was in Shanghai. Agent 007 might approach at any moment.

"You Fox?" came a voice from my left.

Startled, I turned to see a small man, around 40 years old. He wore lizard skin shoes, black pants, a black sport coat, and an odd black tie with a two carat faux diamond stud in the middle.

"Gumm?" I whispered. We shook hands.

"I've reserved a table in the back corner," he answered.

He led the way. Soon we sat across from one another, a lone candle flickering on the table between us.

A waitress, carrying a pitcher and glasses, appeared

from behind the curtain. She had a delicate porcelain face and striking dark, almond-shaped eyes. In a moment her exotic accent would fill the air.

"Wudder?" she inquired.

What a pity. The P-burgians already possessed her.

"I'll take a wudder," Gumm proclaimed.

So did I. She poured two wudders. Gumm raised his glass.

"Well, as they say in P-burg, 'Pennsylvania is just 50 cents away'."

We each took a drink, then got down to business.

"Fox, as you probably know, there are two types of Chinese restaurants: those similar to this place, where scores of patrons can enjoy an eat-in dining experience. Then there are the cramped standing-room-only take-out eateries such as the Green Lotus. The large restaurants maintain a sizable staff and are owned and operated by easily identifiable individuals. Not necessarily so with the take-out places."

The reason for today's meeting was starting to unfold.

"Suppose, Mr. Fox, you decided next week to move with your wife and small child to Peking, China so that you could start up a little take-out restaurant serving American fare. Do you think you'd make it?"

"Of course not," I said. "I don't speak Chinese. I wouldn't have the slightest idea how to negotiate a lease, transfer the working capital necessary to buy cooking equipment, telephones, or supplies. I'd be a fish out of water."

"How, then, is it possible," offered Gumm, "for penniless Chinese immigrants who speak no English to arrive in this country on Monday, and to open a restaurant by Tuesday afternoon? Where does the $300,000 start-up capital come from? How do they gross $1 million the first year when other similar businesses fail?"

I didn't answer.

"Ever hear of the Chinese Mafia?"

"Yes, but when I think Chinese Mafia, I think New York, Chicago, L.A.," I said.

"Well, think a little closer to home," Gumm suggested. "Think Wynslow Township."

Gumm had my attention.

"The drill is simple, Fox. The Mafia extricates a young family from China. In return, the family works to the bone from sunrise to sunset. They get a place to eat and sleep. The mob sets up the lease, buys the equipment, and keeps the profits.

"It ain't like the Italian Mafia," Gumm continued. "Big cars. Flashy suits. Constant interviews with the press. With the Italians, if there's a problem, they invite you to a nice pasta-and-wine dinner, they shoot you and then cry at the church funeral. Later on, the hit man does 30 years at Lewisburg. With the Chinese Mafia, it's a little different. If there's a problem they just shoot you. No dinner, no crying, no church."

"Why are you telling me all of this?"

"Why? To convince you to let go of some chicken shit township business privilege tax. This thing is bigger than you and Wynslow Township. Understand? The Green Lotus is connected directly to the mob and the Big Man himself."

"Big Man?"

Gumm looked left, and then right. He inched closer to the flickering candle in the middle of the table. He whispered two words:

"Binney Wang."

"Binney Wang?" I repeated out loud.

Gumm's face became distressed as he waved his arms. "Shhh!"

I looked to the left and right. Then I apologized.

"Wudder?"

We both jumped out of our seats. Thankfully, it was just our waitress appearing from behind a glass beaded curtain.

"You gents ready to order?"

- - - - - - - - - - - - - - - - - - - -

Thursday evening was the monthly meeting of the township commissioners. The Green Lotus' uncollected business privilege tax was, for the fifth consecutive month, listed on the agenda.

As usual, the meeting began with courtesy of the floor, that wonderful moment in a democracy when ordinary citizens can voice their concerns. It's precisely why totalitarian dictatorships have maintained appeal throughout the ages. Old Mrs. Lilly once again took control of the microphone.

"We got more of them weeds growin' near 5th and Turner. What are you going to do about it?" she demanded as she smacked her 80-year-old left fist into her 80-year-old right palm. The commissioners all looked in my direction for a response.

"I have a call into the weedologist," I assured Mrs. Lilly.

"Well, let's get a move-on. Them weeds ain't gonna walk away themselves," she barked.

There followed a discussion regarding the rising number of Canada geese frequenting the township park without permission, and the need for a roller blading ordinance.

"I believe that concludes Courtesy of the Floor," Commissioner Goodheart noted. "At this time, the five commissioners will meet with the township solicitor to discuss pending litigation."

The spectators, including Mrs. Lilly and her four-wheeled aluminum walker, filed out of the room. Commissioner Pompagass and the panel of elected officials instinctively began to focus their attention on me.

"Any progress with the Green Lotus tax issue, Counselor?" Commissioner Filum inquired. The room grew quiet as I rose to my feet.

"You may recall I was unable to locate the actual owner of the restaurant. Without that information, it's difficult to file a complaint claiming a tax is due."

"So ... ?" Commissioner Filum prodded impatiently.

"So ... " I began, "simply put, the restaurant may be owned by the Mafia."

Commissioner Goodheart was incredulous. "The Italians are running a Chinese restaurant?"

"No, Commissioner. The *Chinese* Mafia."

"The Chinese have a mafia?" Commissioner Eldridge blurted out. He was a local issues kind of guy.

"They tend to keep a low profile," I noted. "They usually don't feed you before killing you."

"But who exactly owns this restaurant?" Filum persisted.

I looked to the right, and then to the left. Although we were in private executive session, I felt an eerie and sinister presence.

"Binney Wang," I whispered.

"Benny Hill?" Goodheart repeated.

"Not Benny, sir. It's Binney. Binney Wang."

"Sounds like what happens when a piston falls out of a cheap foreign car," Commissioner Eldridge noted as he laughed out loud. Some of the other commissioners joined him. I didn't. It was time to give some sound advice.

"Commissioners, I question the wisdom of pursuing this tax. What we have here is the head of a rather extensive organized crime family. I don't think it would be prudent to trouble a mobster over a tax, the total of which probably doesn't exceed $1,500."

The possible loss of any money did not sit well with Commissioner Filum. He took exception to my suggestion, as he thumbed through several pages attached to his clipboard.

"Just a minute, there, Fox. If my calculations are correct, the township has already paid you $435 to pursue this matter. And there's a bill from Metro Detective Agency of New York. We have paid a Detective Gumm $650. Does that sound about right?"

"It does. But Binney Wang is a highly dangerous - "

"Now, Mr. Fox," Filum interrupted, "the township

has already spent $1,085 to collect $1,500, the latter sum of which still hasn't been retrieved. Don't you think the commissioners of Wynslow Township have an obligation to the taxpayers of this municipality to pursue this matter?"

The other four commissioners' heads were bobbing up and down in affirmation. I would have to pursue the elusive Binney Wang.

I drafted a letter on nondescript township stationery and addressed it to the office located on the 38th floor of the Empire State Building. The letter requested in a diplomatic manner that Binney tender the business privilege tax due, plus accruing penalties and interest. Formal legal action was inferred if timely payment was not received. At the conclusion of this unsigned letter, I typed "Very truly yours - the Township of Wynslow". I felt relieved that my name and whereabouts had not fallen into the wrong hands.

- - - - - - - - - - - - - - - - - - -

"There's a Binney Wang here to see you," my receptionist announced nonchalantly, even though this could possibly have been both my last appointment and the last day of my life.

I've never liked walk-ins - this one not withstanding. I gathered myself as I glanced out my back window. There was a spotless, top-of-the-line-you-need-a-bodyguard-to-drive-this-bad-boy Mercedes in the parking lot, positioned next to my rusted Buick. I proceeded to the reception area, wondering if I were walking to my death. Did I have a Last Will and Testament? Had I bothered to sign it? Would the drafter of my obituary remember to include that in my prime, I was a national champion boomerang thrower? It didn't matter, for I had begun to open the door.

There looming before me towered the tallest, meanest looking Asian I had ever had the misfortune to meet. My knees began to shake.

"Mr. Wang, I presume," I squeaked.

A diminutive Asian man, smaller than I, stepped out

from behind the silent giant. "No, I am Binney Wang," he said, "but when you are not so big, it is best to bring a friend."

Some friend! The silent bodyguard looked like the dance partner for the Bride Of Frankenstein.

"Won't you come back to my office," I heard myself say.

"Thank you," Binney responded politely.

They followed me into my private domain. I was nervous. My throat was dry. I needed a drink.

"Would you care for some water?" I asked.

"Wudder would be nice," Binney confirmed.

"I'll be right back," I promised, as I rose to my feet. I walked out of the room to the wudder cooler in the hallway, and soon realized the bodyguard had followed me. He watched as I poured two wudders, and then we both returned to our seats and to Binney. Mr. Wang didn't waste much time getting to the point. People in chauffeur-driven Mercedes usually don't.

Only one other person I can recall had ever visited my office in a chauffeured vehicle. He had been in a rush, too. A couple years back, some pompous lawyer from Philadelphia came up here for depositions. He arrived in a chauffeur-driven Cadillac. I asked him how he could afford such opulence.

"Don't be naïve," he huffed. "I charge $500 an hour. The car and driver cost just $100 an hour. I work. Someone else drives. What's not to like?"

I can't wait until I, too, can charge $500 an hour. But I digress. Binney wanted to focus upon the issue at hand.

"I got your letter threatening legal action if I don't pay the township's business privilege tax." He took a sip of the spring wudder.

"But I didn't sign the letter. How did you know to come here?"

Binney smiled. "I know everything. You are very persistent. I could use a lawyer like you. I came to see if you will work for me. I pay better than the township."

I hadn't been both this flattered and terrified since Joanne Dingerlacher asked me to the senior prom.

"But you hardly know me," I stammered.

"I know everything about you," Binney corrected. "Everything. You were once a boomerang throwing champion."

I wondered if he knew whether I ended up taking Joanne to the prom. I wondered if he knew I was about to shit my pants.

"I pay well for team players. I'll start you out at $20,000 a week, plus bonuses."

Twenty thousand a week! Last month my banker turned me down for a $10,000 line of credit with my house as collateral.

I took a nervous sip of wudder. At that salary, I might not have to accept any more stop sign violation cases where I begged for a $50 retainer.

"You'll give me your answer now, Mr. Fox. I am a very busy man."

"Don't do it!" this little voice whispered in my right ear. I looked to my side, and saw a 3-inch angel perched precariously on my shoulder. Once in a while her silky wings fluttered as she tried to maintain her balance. "When he tires of you, he'll grind you up as won ton stuffing. You'd make a lousy mobster anyway. We both know you're a sissy la la."

"That's a cool half mil a year, pal" came a persuasive voice from my left. "And this guy don't pay taxes, so *you* don't pay taxes. Get it?"

There on my opposite shoulder sat a flame-red 3-inch tall fast-talking salesman with a pitchfork tail.

"Tick tock, Fox," said the devil. "Opportunity only knocks once."

"My bodyguard here owns three hotels in the Cayman Islands," Binney interrupted. "You'll do O.K., too."

The glum giant shook his head up and down.

Binney could see the hesitation in my eyes. After all, he knew everything about me. I wouldn't do it.

"Pity, Mr. Fox." He pulled a check out of his pocket and signed it in Chinese block characters. He pushed it across the table in my direction. It was a draft in the sum of $1,648.50, made payable to the Township of Wynslow.

"Here's the business privilege tax for last year - to the penny. The township will receive a similar check each year from now on. But Mr. Fox, don't pursue me again. That would be ... foolish."

Binney reached in another pocket and handed me a solid black tie with a familiar diamond stud in the middle.

"Your Detective Gumm must have ... dropped this by accident."

Binney and his bodyguard stood up. Wang held out a hand. I shook it. In less than a minute, they and the Mercedes were gone.

I called the detective agency the next morning to tell Gumm his tie had been found.

"Gumm? He's been missing for three weeks," his secretary stammered.

Those $50 retainers didn't look so bad after all.

CHAPTER FOUR:
THE MENTAL HEALTH HEARING

Only three months after passing the Bar, I was appointed to the local Public Defender staff. I began to represent indigent individuals accused of one crime or another. The county taxpayers covered my fees. My experience as a criminal defense attorney was limited, but that didn't bother the majority of poor wretches I represented, since most of them had very little experience as criminals. For them, it was like getting a free haircut at the local cosmetology school - you got what you paid for.

There was one notable exception. Daniel Toth peered at me with skeptical eyes as he sat behind iron bars at the Northampton County Prison. Although I was assigned to represent him, the alleged armed robber failed to transmit the usual enthusiasm generated by the incarcerated when someone - anyone - shows up to offer assistance.

"How long you been practicing, Stud?"

I looked behind me. No one was there, so I decided he must be talking to me. "About three months," I bragged.

My answer may not have given Toth the assurance he sought. That night, he tied some bedsheets together, and slipped over the prison wall. His case is still pending.

As part of my new duties, I was assigned to represent defendants involuntarily incarcerated at the local mental hospital where their court proceedings took place. It was convenient for the patients and the medical staff alike. Back in the 1970s, when the shad actually swam up the Delaware River to spawn, and there were no traffic jams on Route 22, the county judicial system functioned with just two judges, the personalities of whom were like night and day. Every Tuesday, the tipstaff, stenographer, one of the judges and I would carpool to the state hospital. One week stately Judge Palmer would serve; the next it was unassuming Judge Grifo.

The construction of the state hospital was one architectural afterthought foisted upon another. There was the stone-sided really old section with iron bars on each window. Attached to that was the old section built of disintegrating red brick. That portion was connected to the main area and had 1920s cement blocks and fake columns. Each of these sections, though, was dwarfed by the new addition constructed during the 1960s. No matter from what angle you looked, everything about the place was depressing. And the smells and sounds originating from within scared me.

My job was simple: I represented the indigent patients involuntarily detained to determine if they posed a threat to themselves or others. I was batting 1,000: I had, during my first three months on the job, failed to secure the release of a single client.

It was a crisp fall day, and it was Palmer's week to conduct hearings. Hinkelberger, the tipstaff, parked the car in a space reserved for doctors, and quickly exited the vehicle, sprinting around the front bumper to open the door for His Honor. Matilda Kromer, the court stenographer, and I, fended for ourselves. We entered the sparse lobby of the hospital and were soon met by the assistant administrator, Mrs. Applebee.

"Mr. Wirthheimer was brought here two days ago, Your Honor," she explained. "He claims to have heard voices commanding him to rid O'Shaugnessy's Pub of any patron who was drinking. He entered the pub on Mechanic Street with a butcher knife and stabbed four people, three of them seriously. He continues, at this time, to be aggressive, disoriented, and uncontrollable."

The judge was unimpressed. "Is he properly constrained?"

"Yes," Mrs Applebee assured him.

"Then let's bring in Mr. Wirthheimer and see if he should remain here as a guest of the commonwealth," Judge Palmer suggested.

I looked at the entrance door to the lunchroom. I could hear the squeaky rubber tire noise of an approaching wheelchair as it glided along the polished floor. It was Mr. Wirthheimer's entourage: a large male attendant, a doctor, and a nurse. My client was seated in the wheelchair, and dressed in faded orange overalls. It would have been difficult for even his mother to have identified him, since his mouth was sealed shut with masking tape, his arms were restrained in a white strait jacket, and his feet were shackled to the wheelchair. Once in a while, he would make grunting sounds. Sometimes his eyes appeared to pop out of the sockets.

"Do you need time to talk with your client?" Judge Palmer asked.

I stared at Palmer in disbelief, then at the restrained mummy struggling in front of me.

"Hi," I stammered. "I'm Larry Fox, your attorney."

Mr. Wirthheimer grunted something. His eyes started to bulge again.

"OK," Judge Palmer announced. "I guess we can get started. Court is now in session."

Dr. Izabad Blazundak testified regarding the patient's present state of mental health, or to be more precise, the alleged lack thereof. I don't know what exactly the good doctor said, since he testified in a Pakistani dialect. When the doctor stopped babbling, Judge Palmer opened his eyes again.

"Very well. If that concludes the direct examination, you may inquire, Mr. Fox."

I gave it my best shot. "Doctor?"

"Ka?"

"Tell me - do you believe my client is presently a

danger to himself or others?"

"Ka. He almos kull fo pippels wid a nif."

"Thank you." That concluded my brilliant cross-examination.

The judge turned to the attendant who was still standing next to my client's wheelchair. He was a giant. He had to duck through the doorway when he entered the room, and from the size of his abdominal girth, he hadn't missed a meal in the last 15 years.

"Orderly," Palmer commanded, "remove the tape from Mr. Wirthheimer's mouth. We need to place any statement he may wish to make on the record."

The orderly palmed the top of Wirthheimer's head, and with his other hand, took hold of the edge of the tape. He repositioned his feet for balance, then ripped the tape off my client's mouth. A portion of the patient's lips were still attached to the tape. The judge pressed forward.

"Is there anything you'd like to say, sir?"

Wirthheimer's eyes stopped bulging for a moment as he felt his lips with his tongue to inventory what might be left.

"You bet there is, Judge!" He stared at me, as he thrust his head in my direction. "First, Your Honor, I paid this here public defender nothin', and nothin' is what I got for a defense."

The judge leaned in my direction.

"He sounds pretty sane to me," he whispered. "If he doesn't say another word, there may be adequate grounds to discharge him."

Wirthheimer's eyes began to grow bigger again. "Second, when I get outta here, Your Honor, I'm going to come looking for *you*, and it won't be a social call. Got it?"

My heart started to pound. Judge Palmer, on the other hand, didn't miss a beat.

"Look all you like. My name is Judge Richard Grifo. I'm in the book."

With those words, Judge Palmer signed an Order of Court detaining Wirthheimer at the hospital for further indefinite observation. He motioned for us to leave, and within minutes the stenographer, the tipstaff, His Honor, and I were on our way back to the courthouse. In the car, I sat stunned and confused. The judge noted my sense of consternation as I gazed out the window not really seeing the passing scenery.

"Anything wrong, counselor?"

"Well ... frankly, Your Honor, I'm surprised."

"At what?"

"You gave that raving lunatic Judge Grifo's name. What if - "

"Nonsense," Judge Palmer assured me, with the wave of his hand. "No chance. First of all, that nut Wirthheimer probably won't get out of the hospital or jail for years. By then, Grifo will have undoubtedly retired and moved to Florida. Now let's look at this logically. By failing to give that maniac my name, I was better able to concentrate on the case. At the same time, Judge Grifo doesn't have to worry, since he never heard the threat in the first place. It's a win-win situation as long as we all know enough to keep this as our little secret."

I looked at the other two passengers - both nodding in silent acquiescence. The judge had taught me an invaluable lesson in what he called Judicial Prudence.

About a month later, I attended a similar hearing at the hospital during which Judge Grifo presided. My client, who had killed someone with a sledge hammer, was being held at the hospital for observation.

"What's your name?" the crazy loon yelled as he struggled in his strait jacket and leg constraints. Judge Grifo didn't hesitate.

"Judge Clinton B. Palmer. I'm in the book."

CHAPTER FIVE:
THE SAFE-CRACKER

During the summer I turned eight, my parents sent me away to music camp. It was a life-altering experience. From my vantage point perched upon the ornate piano bench, my legs dangling above the pedals, the patient instructors taught me wondrous things - the least of which was that baseball can only be played during a relatively short period of one's life, but a musician doesn't actually reach his artistic prime for decades. And I discovered that the more important a person was, the shorter was his or her name, such as Tiger, Madonna, Zeus, or God.

Music camp is where I first met the great Vaska. To this day, I don't know if that was his first or last name, but it was the only appellation that he acknowledged.

"It's Vaska," we would all whisper among ourselves with both anticipation and awe whenever the maestro entered the recital hall to grace his fortunate students with both his wisdom and artistry. We may have been young, but we knew we were in the presence of a greatness that required our obedience and respect.

Vaska was unpretentious and soft-spoken, with a thick Transylvanian-Bela Lugosi accent. He was a bizarre man. But I wouldn't have wanted it otherwise. After all, he was a world-famous cellist who had escaped, as rumor had it, from a far-off place called Prussia.

It was his posture, however, that grasped our collective attention. Never before had I seen a hunchback, much less a nonagenarian, with disheveled locks of pure white hair cascading in disarray upon his disfigured and brutally bent shoulders. He was oblivious to the ravages of his outward appearance as he shuffled along, his head lowered toward the ground. He was intent upon beginning the morning's class on time.

The most astonishing feature of the genius now stooped in our presence was his arms. The left appendage did not hang by his side. Rather, it curved by some overpowering and cruel design toward his belt buckle. His right arm hung in suspended animation, outstretched, as if it was grasping some unseen object from out of the air. It was clear poor Vaska had not experienced a comfortable moment in years, so arduous and labored was his entry into the classroom.

His doting wife, Natasha, his constant companion, stood erect and silent by his side, holding his cello, an instrument she would have protected with her very life. She carried out his every wish in loving obedience. She was 30 years his junior, but there was an unspoken bond between them that was unmistakable. He stared directly at the floor, which loomed only three feet from his animated eyes.

"Mein cello, bitte," Vaska requested, as he gently nestled his frail body into the rehearsal chair that faced us.

His wife unhesitatingly obliged. She approached her husband with the one thing that had been his unfaltering traveling companion through nine decades and two World Wars - his scratched, discolored, priceless cello. In this seated position, his two disfigured arms curved inward toward each other. His wife slowly lifted the ancient wooden instrument, and with the patience and skill of a surgeon, gingerly lowered the cello between the encircling arms of the artist, until the bottom of the cello made gentle contact with the ground.

Instantly, the caterpillar was transformed into the most exotic of butterflies, for Vaska had now come alive. In a heartbeat, his tormented body caressed the beloved instrument, as if it and his bent frame had been designed for but one thing. His left hand, with bow at the ready, was joined in music-making by the right, and now effortlessly touched the upper strings. In a word, Vaska, who had played his cello about 10 hours each day during his entire life, had taken on the permanent posture of someone seated at the cello. He had become the cello. The cello had become him.

And as he played, we sat in stunned silence. How could such beautiful tones issue forth from a mere piece of wood? How could such a crippled body produce such virtuosic magic?

"Can't you feel the electricity in the air?" Susie, the 12- year-old clarinetist, whispered to me. I could, and do to this very day.

- - - - - - - - - - - - - - - - - - - -

"Uncle Seymour died yesterday."

And with that solemn pronouncement, my convoluted odyssey began.

Seymour Heimsoth had been my client for as long as I could remember. He had inherited his father's 100-acre dairy farm over 30 years ago, and had faithfully continued the family business. For him, dairy farming was a way of life. The cows were milked every morning, and they never took kindly to strange or unknown hands. As a result, Seymour, who lived alone, never left the farm for as much as a single day. No vacations in Hawaii. No days of rest on Christmas or Easter. He finally worked himself to death at age 73.

His nephew, Stewart, found the body in the large, red milking barn. After calling the coroner, he contacted me. Stewart, who graduated from high school 20 years earlier, had since been working in the neighborhood hardware store. He was pleasant and honest but unsophisticated regarding the administration of an estate. He was Seymour's closest relative and friend.

"I'm sorry for your loss," I advised him.

"Thank you for your thoughts," Stewart responded genuinely and politely. "Tell me, did my uncle have a last will or something?"

As a matter of fact, he did, and I had written it. I remember having to obtain the information out in the barn while Seymour milked the herd. He simply didn't have the time to come to my office. After I drafted the document, I returned to the farm so Seymour could sign the papers.

"I got a good place to keep the will," he said with an air of finality.

He led me down his basement steps and pointed toward the coal bin. There in the light created by a single dangling incandescent bulb, stood a safe - not just any old 100 pound fireproof $75 pop-it-in-the-trunk-of-your-car safe. This depository was bigger than a side-by-side refrigerator-freezer. It stood about seven feet high, and must have weighed more than three tons. A complex crystal timing device with a large brass combination tumbler projected from the silver and chrome polished doors. At the top of this silent metallic monster appeared ornate words in hand-painted gold leaf lettering: *Hoover Safe Company - 1878 - Chicago*.

"I'll put them papers in here with my other important stuff," he confided.

I was astonished. The wooden steps leading to the basement had groaned and bent under my weight as I had descended, and there was no other entrance or exit. Where did this safe come from, and how did it get down here?

"That's a good story," my host confirmed. "You see, my great-grandfather didn't believe in banks or nothin' since one failed once and took all his money. So when he recovered and decided to build this farmhouse, he dug the basement first, bought the safe, had it shipped here from Illinois and lowered it into the hole. Then he built the farmhouse above it. Great-grandpa figured, if anyone ever wanted to take his safe, they'd have to remove the house first."

He was right. Great-grandpa, then grandpa, then pa, and finally Seymour had all enjoyed the uninterrupted use of the safe.

- - - - - - - - - - - - - - - - - - - -

Stewart was still patiently waiting for an answer.

"Yes, Stewart, there was a last will and testament. I believe Seymour kept it in his basement safe."

"More than likely. By any chance, do you have a copy?" he wondered.

I checked my old file and returned to the conversation. "Yes, I have an unsigned copy - only the original will would have been signed."

"Does it say who is the xator?"

"You mean 'executor'?"

"Yeah. That's it. The executor."

"The will appoints you, Stewart."

"I thought so. See, my uncle always told me I was his favorite relative. He did say at one point that he put me in his will to oversee his estate. Now what do we do?"

"We need to get the original will out of that safe," I advised him. "Do you know the combination?"

Silence.

"Not really," Stewart sighed. "You see, Uncle Seymour - he always said that when the time was right, he'd pass on the combination to the safe. I guess time got to him before he picked the right time. Ain't there locksmiths who open safes? I got the feelin' there may be other collectibles stashed in there, too."

Stewart's point was well taken. As the representative of the estate, he was now tasked with the responsibility of inventorying the assets owned by his deceased uncle. The over-sized vault had to be opened. With his permission, I agreed to locate a professional safe-cracker.

That afternoon, I scoured the phone book. Let's see ..."saddlery" ... "safety shoes" ... "sandblasting" ... here it is..."safes and vaults - opening and repairing." The ad ended on a hopeful note: "We usually leave our drill in the truck." There was an 800 number and a dry directive: "Ask for Gushty." For all I knew, I might have been calling

Kalamazoo. I dialed the number; someone picked up.

"Gushty."

"Hello, this is Lawrence Fox."

"Vhat?"

"LAWRENCE FOX," I yelled.

"Du I know you?"

"No. Do you open safes?"

"Vhat?"

"SAFES!" I screamed. "DO YOU OPEN SAFES?"

"Yah. Are you stuck in vun now?"

"No."

"Gut. I hate emergencies. Call me in vun veek."

"Wait! Where are you located?"

"Vhy? You coming vid de safe to here?"

"No, it's too big."

"Vhat?"

"THE SAFE IS VERY BIG", I yelled.

"OK. Better maybe I come der."

The next 10 minutes of conversation were equally disjointed and rambling. I was confident, though, that I had secured Gushty's arrival at the farm at noon on the following Saturday. I described the gold lettering and the date embossed on the safe. I told Stewart about the safe-cracker and his repair shop located somewhere in the Pocono Mountains.

"Can I be there when he comes to the farmhouse?" the executor inquired.

"You are the representative of the estate," I advised him. "You have as much right to be there as anyone."

"A few relatives and friends have been calling about poor Uncle Seymour. Can they tag along?"

"I suppose so, if they stay out of the way. The locksmith may have to drill the safe open."

"O.K.," Stewart assured me. "I'll see you Saturday."

- - - - - - - - - - - - - - - - - - - -

The farm hadn't changed, minus the cows. Stewart

had thoughtfully made arrangements to have the herd moved to a neighboring farm for proper care and safety. I arrived early at about 11 o'clock, but three cars were already parked along the winding lane leading to the house. Stewart met me on the front porch and began the introductions.

"This here is Freda, Uncle Seymour's second cousin. And that's her husband, Albert. And over there is Bertram, Seymour's nephew from Wisconsin, and his wife, Faye."

I shook hands with everyone, including Stewart's friend, Hal, who also worked at the hardware store. Then we all went inside. The kitchen and dining room were sparse in decor, as were the upstairs bedroom and bath. If Seymour had any significant assets, it wasn't apparent from a survey of his living quarters.

As I stood gazing at a portrait of Seymour's mother, a sepia hanging in the hallway, Faye approached me from behind.

"Excuse me, sir. Some of us have traveled a fair distance. Could you tell me when you plan to have the 'Reading of the Will'?"

It was the same question that had been posed dozens of times by other potential beneficiaries of other estates. I was about to respond, but we were interrupted by the noise of screeching brakes and a shot muffler. I excused myself and proceeded to the front porch.

An old man struggled to emerge from a battered black panel truck. He was at least 85 years old, and was burdened with a hunched back. He gingerly slid his feet from the driver's seat to the ground.

"Who's that?" Faye asked Bertram.

"I dunno," he responded, "but he ain't from the Wisconsin side of the family."

I maneuvered through the onlookers, now gathered on the porch, and approached the visitor.

"Gushty?"

"Vhat?"

It was Gushty, alright. His tangled white hair flowed in strands about his disfigured shoulders. He struggled to shut the panel truck door, and then stood transfixed, his body bent toward the ground.

"Damn," he muttered.

"Is there a problem?" I inquired.

"I tink I just locked my keys in de damned truck!"

"That shouldn't be much of a problem," I assured him.

"Really? You get dem out?"

"No, I mean you're a locksmith ... "

Gushty attempted without success to straighten himself sufficiently to look me in the eye.

"Son - I'm a safe-cracker - not a car-jacker. Call de triple A again. Deh hate ven I call dem. You gut cell phone?"

Gushty made the call, and then turned to me. "Hopefully, I von't need my drills or blasting caps. Let's look at de safe."

"It's in the cellar," I explained.

"Vhat?"

"THE BASEMENT!" I yelled.

"O.K. Lead de veh."

I journeyed down the cellar steps, followed by Gushty, Stewart, and the entourage of relatives and friends. The hanging bulb once again illuminated the huge safe. Gushty's ancient eyes grew transfixed with anticipation as his arthritic legs slowly transported him across the dirt floor. Methodically, he placed both hands on the polished chrome exterior doors, as he positioned his ear near the tumbler mechanism. Someone on the Wisconsin side of the family sneezed. Gushty frowned.

"I must have absolute quiet," he instructed. "Heavy breathers go avay!"

I stopped breathing. So did everyone else. Gushty took a small quantity of emery paper from his left trouser pocket, and gently began to sand the fingertips of his right hand. As he did, he miraculously moved with the grace of a cat to the left side of the safe, and began tapping the polished metal with his knuckle. Once in a while he would cock his head, similar to an anteater looking for termites. He moved to the back of the safe, all the while sanding his fingertips. He placed his ear to the steel back of the repository, and stood motionless for what seemed an eternity. No one inhaled or exhaled, lest they be banished to the first floor.

The old man moved to the right side again, and while touching his thumbs together, pushed with both palms of his hands against the steel panel. Then he returned to the front of the vault, and stared at the tumbler as he continued to sand one particular spot on his right pinkie finger. A spider was spinning a web in a rafter overhead. I hoped the noise of its weaving would not break Gushty's concentration.

He inched toward the tumbler and pressed his left hand upon the left side of the safe. Ever so gently, he carefully positioned his right thumb and third finger and began to turn the ancient dial. At the same time, he pressed his right ear to the safe.

There was an electricity, an excitement, in the air. Gushty no longer appeared to be disfigured. For one defining moment, I was eight years old again, and it was as if Vaska again performed before me. Gushty had become one with the safe. So often had he performed, that his skeletal system had slowly been reshaped to enfold the safe he now embraced. He was the artist. We were his amazed students.

He turned the combination dial a mere centimeter, listening for the music of internal clicking tumblers. Through his fingertips and ears, he could peer past the chrome and silver door, into the very gears and locking mechanisms lying deep within.

Gushty methodically turned the tumbler. Then he slowly stood as erect as his body would permit. The spider stopped spinning, for Gushty was about to grasp the brass handle on the exterior door. Perspiration was streaming from his forehead. He gave the handle a gentle twist, and amazingly, the metal hatch swung open. Faye started to breathe for the first time in 15 minutes. Some of the relatives broke into spontaneous applause. Gushty took a deep bow. Everyone, including the spider, strained to peek into the dark confines of the repository.

A collection of the back side of several animated heads began bobbing and weaving in front of me, jostling for position. I couldn't see a thing.

"Stand back, everyone," Freda ordered. "You're blocking the light!"

Albert produced a small cigarette lighter and lit it. The dancing flame generated minor illumination.

"And you wanted me to stop smoking," he scolded Freda, who elbowed the others in order to protect her turf near the entrance to the safe.

Faye had been edged backward into the second row of mourners. This involuntary relocation displeased her.

"Damn it! We came all the way from Wisconsin! Move over!"

Hal and Stewart comprised the third row of onlookers. Gushty and I were relegated to the fourth.

"It looks like a lota stuff in there," Freda announced.

"For the love of Pete, Albert, can't you hold that damn lighter steady?"

That was enough. I had agreed these relatives could be present, but not for a feeding frenzy, an act that dishonored the memory of the decedent, and endangered the orderly accounting of the contents of the safe. I needed to reclaim control of the situation.

"Pardon me," I apologized as I waded forward. Freda was the last to relinquish her territorial claim. Standing with my back to the vault, I turned to address the agitated spectators.

"People ... Your conduct is inappropriate and your presence here serves no purpose."

Admonished, Albert slowly began to lower the flame of his lighter. Freda closed her mouth, which just about killed her. Faye was livid.

"Well, in Wisconsin, guests are treated with hospitality," she blared.

I spotted Gushty standing next to Hal back in the fourth row of faces. "Did you get the combination?"

"Yah."

"So if we lock it back up, it can be opened later?"

"Yah."

"Then do so now," I instructed.

Gushty inched forward as the disappointed spectators shuffled up the creaky basement stairs. With a snap of the handle, and a quick twist of the tumbler, the safe was again secured. The spider, realizing that nothing further would be gained by hanging around, climbed back up its silken thread. I was the last to leave the cellar, so I shut off the light and closed the door.

A "Triple A" tow truck had just pulled into the driveway. Gushty made his way to the young driver who stood next to the vehicle. He was dressed in greasy overalls.

"Did you call for service?" the kid inquired.

"Vhat?"

"Did you call Triple A?"

"Yah."

"What's the problem, sir?"

"My keys. Dey are locked in de truck," Gushty explained.

"Not a problem," the kid assured us. "I'll have 'em out in a minute." He returned to his vehicle for some tools.

Gushty and I now stood alone in the front yard facing each other. We were about to have a conversation I'd remember for the rest of my life.

"So, how much do I owe you?"

"Let's see," Gushty calculated. "Fordy-five minutes on de road, and den a half hour here, and fordy-five minutes back to home. But I didn't have to blast or drill. You pay me today, not to send an estate check in a month or two, and I'll charge you just tree hundred dollar."

Seemed fair to me. I would have gladly paid more. I began to write a check. Gushty decided to return the favor.

"Fox ... "

I looked up from my check writing. "Yes?"

"Dat lady, Faye, is valking over here."

"Not again," I sighed.

"Listen to me - der isn't much time. Ven she asks about de Reading of de Last Vill and Testament, take my lead. Understand?"

No, I didn't. But for some reason, I did as he said. Faye tapped me on the back of the shoulder.

"Pardon me for interrupting," she began, "but could you tell me when you plan to conduct the Reading of the Will? As I may have mentioned, we came all the way from Wisconsin. I need to know so we can book our return flight."

"De Reading takes place vithin tventy-four hours after de Vill is found," Gushty confirmed. "De Vill is in de safe, so de Reading vill occur here at de farmhouse tomorrow in de evening. Isn't dat so, Attorney Fox?"

I studied Gushty's ancient face. There was a quiet wisdom in his eyes, similar to Vaska's countenance. I turned to Faye.

"The Reading will take place tomorrow night promptly at 8. Formal dress is requested, but not mandatory."

Faye thanked me, and withdrew quickly to tell the others. Gushty smiled at me.

"You like vatching movies?" he questioned.

"If there's no violence," I responded, not knowing where he was going with this.

"If I've seen vun movie, I've seen terty dat depict some lawyer sitting at de head of de large table, vid all de grieving relatives seated facing him as he reads de Last Vill and Testament. Now you and I both know dat der is no such ting, and dat such scenes are de figment of some screenwriter's imagination ... "

Gushty was, of course, correct. No lawyer has ever engaged in such a ridiculous exercise. When a will is found, written notice of an interest in the estate is simply mailed to the named beneficiaries.

"But people like de Faye, dey vatch de movies, dey tink you got to read de Vill. Sometimes it is vise not to disappoint dose who eagerly avait your services," Gushty explained.

"I'm not following," I responded, as I handed him a check for his labors, a draft made payable to *Gushty*.

"Vake up, Fox! You not de stupid. Do you qvestion ven I show up here half deaf, and yet I demand dat de Miss Faye stop breating so I vill hear de click of de gear in de safe vit tree inch steel valls?"

"Well, I figured you must have put your ear real close to the - "

"And it seem a little strange, no, dat I vill open safes all day, but I not to unlock de truck myself for de keys ... "

"Now that you mention it, I was a little surprised that -"

"You vill listen, yah?" Gushty interrupted. "Is dis check goot?"

"Yes, it won't bounce. You can cash it today."

"Yes, yes. And dat's vhy I like you. I'm de 87 years old, and let you in on de little secret: Illusion. It's all de illusion!"

"I beg your - "

"Opening de safe. Just a show. See, in de movies, vhenever someone breaks into de safe, de guy sand de fingertips, listen for de clicking. Dats de stuff of de Superman!"

"Den ... I mean *then* how did you open the safe?" I stammered.

Gushty reached into his right pants pocket and after producing some emery paper, located a small disintegrating leather-bound book held together with a rubber band. He handed me the ancient treatise. I read the title:

Hoover Safe Company Combinations.

"De Hoover safes ver manufactured from de 1870 to de 1920. Tousands of dem," Gushty explained. "Dis book lists each safe by de serial number, vich den corresponds vid each safe's combination. Ven I vent behind de safe down der, I found de serial number, den I looked in book fer de combination. Listening at de tumbler vas just fer de teatrical effect. I give you now de combination."

He handed me a slip of paper with three numbers on

it.

"Turn left, den right, den left."

"But why all the theatrics?" I begged.

"You don't listen, Fox. I have de lifetime of dealing vid customers like de Miss Faye - some peoples vant an illusion. Vidout it, dey tink you de impostor, 'cause dat's vhat dey learn in de movies. If I hadn't put on such a goot show, vood you have been so villing to write out de check for de tree hundred dollar? I could have given you de combination over de phone."

This lesson alone was well worth the cost of his services. My tutor concluded with the following advice:

"Faye and de oders vant de Reading of de Vill. Accommodate der vishes and you vill have contented clients, unless, of course, dey don't get vhat dey vanted from de dearly departed."

"Hey Mister," the Triple A kid announced as he approached. "I found 'em." He handed the elusive keys to Gushty, who put them, the emery paper, and the little leather book back into his pocket.

"Tanks," he responded to the kid. "You've got a natural talent. Have you ever tot about de career in de safe-cracking?" The kid rolled his eyes as he walked back to his truck.

- - - - - - - - - - - - - - - - - - - -

Nothing in the Pennsylvania Rules of Civil Procedure precluded me from engaging in a Reading of the Will. Just because no sane lawyer had ever actually choreographed such a production before did not suggest that I could not establish a new legal precedent. It happens all the time. I, too, had seen the movies that depicted the decor and the atmosphere that would be expected by the family in mourning. I rented two grotesque Liberace-esque candelabra. I added a recording of mortuary music used by funeral directors during viewings. The final touch was my old tuxedo.

Stewart met me at the farmhouse and followed my lead as we spread a crisp new linen cloth over the dining room table. We dusted off the six matching chairs, lit all 16 candles on the candelabra, and turned out the lights. I flipped on the stiff music and straightened my cummerbund.

"Wow!" Stewart exclaimed. "Did you learn all this at law school?"

I could but smile, for the doorbell chime signaled the arrival of our guests. Freda, Albert, Bertram, and Faye had driven together in Albert's old Cadillac. Faye was the first to push her way through the door. She may have come halfway across the country, but she had brought her very best Reading of the Will wardrobe - a Wisconsin-bought pink and white satin evening gown that shimmered in the soft candlelight. She scanned the room, locked in on the candelabra and shot around to scold Bertram, who was trying not to step on her flowing train.

"See? I told you I wasn't overdressed. Fool. This here's a high class Reading of the Will."

Bertram appeared embarrassed that he had chosen to wear a common blue sports coat and slacks. Freda and Albert brought up the rear, boasting matching polyester pants and sweaters. They were from New Jersey, a state where Will Reading isn't taken quite so seriously.

"Won't you be seated," I suggested in my solemn Will Reading voice. Some unknown musical ensemble played *Nearer My God To Thee* in the background. Bertram pulled out a chair for Faye, as Albert and Freda each independently grabbed a seat. I took my position at the head of the table, where I saw the attentive Stewart peering between the flickering candle flames at the table's other end.

"Dearly beloved," I began, "we are gathered here tonight for the Reading of the Last Will and Testament of Seymour Q. Heimsoth, your friend, relative, and local dairy farmer."

I produced my briefcase from under the table, and placed it near one of the candelabra. Reaching into the leather satchel, I brought forth a legal-size document.

"This is the decedent's Last Will and Testament. I will now commence the reading thereof."

"Good Lord!" Faye whispered to Bertram. "Can't you just feel the electricity in the air? I've never been to a real Reading before!"

We had something in common. Neither had I.

- - - - - - - - - - - - - - - - - - - -

I can still recall my first child support hearing. Judge Weaver heard the case in Courtroom No. 3 of the Northampton County Courthouse. He had presided over 5,000 similar cases spanning a 20 year judicial career. I was fresh out of law school.

I represented Sylvia Trashler, whose estranged husband had left her and their four children, all under the age of nine, so that he could take up residence with his new love, a classy young lass he met in a local bar. His Honor ordered that Mr. Trashler pay on a weekly basis 55 percent of his income to his wife.

"But Judge," my client implored the Court, "that isn't enough. How am I going to raise four kids on that?"

Mr. Trashler had other thoughts. "Your Honor. That's too much. How am I going to live?"

I felt I had failed to represent adequately my client. That afternoon, I passed the judge in the courthouse hallway. His Honor pulled me aside and whispered in my ear.

"Not to worry, son. If both parties leave unhappy, then the court did its job."

- - - - - - - - - - - - - - - - - - - -

I finished reading aloud the contents of the Heimsoth last will and testament. Faye was the first to regain consciousness.

"You mean that's it? Bertram gets the piano? How the hell are we supposed to ship a $50 piece of crap piano back to Wisconsin?"

Freda wasn't happy, either. "I only get the portrait of

his mother? That old bat? I never even liked her. Never. Come on, Albert, let's get the hell out of here."

Freda, Albert, Faye, and Bertram stomped out the front door and into the waiting Cadillac. I could still hear them screaming at each other as they drove away.

Only Stewart remained. But he was fine. "It was a lovely Reading of the Will," he smiled.

"What are you going to do with the farm?" I asked him.

"I'll live here. I think that's what Uncle Seymour would have wanted."

And that's what he did. He left the hardware store, and took up the dairy business. At the end of each month, he put the profits from the sale of milk into the basement safe that conveniently remained with the farmhouse. Combination and all.

CHAPTER SIX:
BUT THAT'S NOT FAIR

Professor Collins' disheveled crop of hair, tossed straight back symphony orchestra conductor-style, made its unannounced entry at the lecture hall door, followed directly underneath by none other than Professor Collins. He may have been 75, but he ascended the podium with ease, beginning his lecture precisely at 9:00 a.m.

This was my first day as a freshman at Villanova Law School and this was the first scheduled class for a new generation of aspiring lawyers. Collins claimed the dubious distinction of being my first law school professor. No doubt the other 218 freshmen shared the same inexperience. My heart raced. Would I cut the mustard in this criminal law lecture, or would I be unmasked as a pretender, flunking out by next Tuesday? Would I end up moving home with my parents? What else would I do with a four-year undergraduate degree in political science?

"Open to page one of your textbook," Collins thundered as his voice, the seasoned instrument of a thousand jury trials, echoed against the back of the lecture hall. "We will consider the case of *Commonwealth versus Armstrong.*"

What was a "Commonwealth"? What was a "versus"? And who was "Armstrong"?

"Now the defendant and his co-conspirator ... "

Defendant? Co-conspirator?

" ... entered a convenience store with the intention of robbing the proprietor at gunpoint. Defendant Armstrong approached the manager of the emporium as he stood at his cash register. There were no other customers present in this old-time general store.

"Armstrong's partner in crime, Fitzpatrick, then brandished a black plastic artificial pistol, similar to that found at any toy store, and waved it at the 70-year-old proprietor who had poor eyesight and a weak heart. Fitzpatrick demanded all the money in the cash register, whereupon the proprietor, believing the gun to be authentic, backed up against some shelving. A 50-pound bag of potatoes fell on the proprietor who suffered a heart attack and died on the spot."

Collins came to a scheduled pause, as he began to study the student roster. Surely we weren't the first class to endure the drill of this particular lecture.

"Where's Adams?"

Dead silence. Had I been Adams, I, too, would have tarried.

"Mr. Adams?"

"Here, sir," came a slight, almost apologetic response. The voice belonged to a red-headed student, who wore a checkered bow-tie. He was Howdy Doody's older brother.

"Adams. How nice of you to join us," said the cat as it played with the mouse. "Tell us, Adams, what crime has Armstrong committed?"

"Crime, sir?"

"Yes, Adams, this is a class in criminal law. Has Armstrong done anything within the four corners of the store, for which he might ultimately face incarceration?"

"Well, I'm not sure."

"Do you plan to charge future clients a $10,000 retainer for that?" Collins asked.

"Actually, sir, my plan was to pursue patent law."

"Tell me, Adams, do you actually believe that you will never meet up with a criminal while engaged in the patent business? Ever hear of 'theft of trade secrets'? Now think, man, what crime has Armstrong committed?"

"Well, he had a gun ... "

"No, Adams, he didn't. His partner, Fitzpatrick, carried the weapon. Focus in on the facts!"

"... but the gun was a toy ... " the struggling Adams interjected.

"Why is that relevant?"

"It means that Fitzpatrick never intended to kill anyone, including the proprietor."

"But the proprietor is dead. Are you suggesting no crime occurred?"

"...Well, they didn't get any money, and there was no actual weapon, and the proprietor had a weak heart to begin with, and it was the proprietor who initially put the bag of potatoes up on the shelf ... "

Collins was growing impatient. He scanned the student list. "Brochius. Mr. Brochius."

"Here, sir," said a 6-foot 5-inch athletic-type sparring partner. He certainly appeared better suited to stand toe-to-toe with the class bully.

"Is there a crime in our midst?" Collins implored.

"There is, sir!"

Collins' ears seemed to perk up and turn, similar to a cat's, as a blood-lust for the hunt enveloped him. "Adams, it appears we have a horse race. Brochius here says there's a crime. Tell us, Mr. Brochius, what's the crime?"

"Some degree of unjustifiable homicide, perhaps murder," Brochius mused, "because, but for the wrongful actions of the defendants, the proprietor would yet be alive, his potatoes still secure on the shelf."

"And so, Brochius, if you were the district attorney, you might indict weaponless Armstrong for murder, based upon the actions of his impetuous partner?"

"Yes. A co-conspirator is to be held equally accountable for the crimes committed by other conspirators."

Brochius clearly wasn't going home to Mommy and Daddy's finished basement.

"Very well, Brochius, turn to page seven of our text, and consider with your fellow neophytes the unfortunate set of facts reported in *State versus Randolph*. In *Randolph*, two would-be armed robbers enter a store, demanding that the manager turn over the contents of the cash register ..."

"Yes, sir."

"... but the store manager has other ideas. He has a working loaded gun of his own which he produces. He chases the two unprepared felons through his establishment. They turn, shoot, and then run toward the exit door as the proprietor returns the fire. But who does the proprietor hit? None other than a poor luckless pedestrian lawfully proceeding along the sidewalk in front of the door. Aged Mrs. McGilicutty dies instantly. But for the attempted robbery by the two co-conspirators, McGilicutty would still be alive. Yet, it was the proprietor with the poor aim who shot the bystander. Are the co-conspirators guilty of murder, District Attorney Brochius?"

"Of course. They should have foreseen that their felonious actions could well have resulted in the death of an innocent third party."

"Do you agree, Mr. Adams?" Collins interjected.

"I don't know," a cautious Adams replied. "It was the proprietor who shot and killed the bystander. The proprietor was under no obligation to discharge his weapon in a crowded store. And he obviously should have known he was a poor marksman, as evidenced by the untimely death of Mrs. McGilicutty. If he had just permitted the police to do their job, rather than choosing to become a self-appointed vigilante, perhaps Mrs. McGilicutty would be alive today."

I was becoming confused. I had tended to agree with Brochius' analysis - until I heard the argument proposed by Adams.

"And so, Mr. Adams, would you consider indicting the proprietor for some form of criminal homicide?" Collins probed.

"I'm not sure."

"District attorneys aren't paid to be indecisive, Adams," Collins scolded. "Perhaps the third case in our textbook might lend further insight into this troubling conundrum. Please turn to page 14 of the text, and consider the case of *Commonwealth versus Gaugler*. In this scenario, we see that the defendant, Gaugler, enters a store with his co-conspirator, Bellini. They intend to rob the proprietor forcibly at gunpoint. But the proprietor activates an audible security alarm that convinces the two criminals they should hastily depart the store. As they flee together out the front door, they are spotted by a police officer on sidewalk foot patrol. The officer calls out for the two criminals to halt, but they ignore the officer's command. The officer then draws his weapon, and shoots one of the fleeing suspects, Bellini, dead; whereupon the other suspect, Gaugler, is quickly taken into custody. Mr. Brochius ..."

"Yes, sir?"

"Would you charge Gaugler with murder?"

The quick-witted Brochius sat quietly, formulating his response. "It was the police officer who shot Bellini dead ..."

"I'm aware of that, Mr. Brochius. But under your analysis, should Gaugler have foreseen that his quest in the store for ill-gotten booty might result in the death of his partner by a third party officer of the law?"

"I suppose so ... They were engaged in criminal activity when they failed to heed the officer's command, an officer who had the right to effectuate an arrest."

Collins returned to his original prey. "Mr. Adams, do you agree that Gaugler committed murder when his partner was shot dead by an officer, and that Gaugler deserves to be executed by the state for his sins?"

"No," Adams protested. "It was the cop, not Gaugler, who killed Bellini. All Gaugler did was attempt a robbery. They didn't even get any loot. Gaugler's no murderer."

The hint of a smile spread across Collins' face. "If I told you that Gaugler was, indeed, executed as a murderer for the death of Bellini, would that cause you some discomfort, Mr. Adams?"

"It wouldn't be fair," Adams said incredulously. "Gaugler didn't kill anyone. He was running away. He shouldn't have paid the supreme price just because some cop happens to shoot his partner after a failed robbery."

Collins, the omnipotent, stopped pacing long enough to stare at his victim.

"FAIR?" the booming voice decreed. "Is that what you said? Listen, Mister, and listen well: If you want fairness and 'nice-nice' wrapped up in a pretty bow, I suggest you become a monk and hereafter reside in a monastery. If you want to learn the law, I invite you to sit here and pay attention."

Having made his point, Collins returned to his lecture podium and textbook, a tome with bent and disheveled pages.

"Mr. Adams appears to be upset by the court-ordered execution of the late and felonious Mr. Gaugler," Collins continued. "Perhaps other bleeding hearts sit sniffling among us. If such is true, the insightful case of *Francis versus Resweber, Sheriff*, might well cause such lightweights, like poor Mr. Adams here, to dare further to question the wisdom of the law. Class, kindly turn your attention to page 94 of the text."

I sat transfixed. In less than half an hour, this 75-year-old, cantankerous S.O.B. had kindled a new fire in my soul. He had posed scores of questions, and had answered none. Was he suggesting that the inquiry, not the response, was the engine of the law? Why was this traveler from a prior century, having been born in 1898, willing to impart a lifetime of insight upon us?

All the while, I thanked God that this sarcastic legal scholar had apparently chosen to pursue his student victims in alphabetical order. Theoretically, I could be spared from public humiliation for another two to three weeks.

We all dutifully turned to page 94. Several undecipherable numbers presented themselves at the top of the case's caption: 329 U.S. 459; 67 S.CT. 374 (1947). I was unwittingly about to enter the realm of United States Supreme Court decisions - edicts from on high from which no further appeals were possible.

Collins possessed the energy of a teenager, as he paced back and forth in front of us.

"Class, let us now consider the fate of one Willie Francis, the petitioner herein, described by the learned justices of our Supreme Court as 'a colored citizen of Louisiana.'

"It's May 3, 1946. World War II has recently drawn to a conclusion. The Sheriff of Saint Martin Parish, Mr. E. L. Resweber, seeks to carry out the September 1945 sentencing of the trial court that has previously determined that Francis, a 17-year-old adolescent, having been found guilty of murder, should be executed for his crime. To comply with the trial court's order, the sheriff has requested that the state's nomadic executioner transport Louisiana's one and only portable electric chair to the local jail where Francis is held.

"On May 3, 1946, the executioner appears at the Saint Martin Parish Jail, driving a beat-up pick-up truck upon which is situated the portable electric chair. Now understand, class, at this point in time, a significant percentage of homes in the South still weren't serviced by electrical power, which was considered a rather new invention.

My attention was riveted upon Collins' every word, as I hastily scanned the Supreme Court decision to which he now referred. Phrases such as "double jeopardy," "equal protection under the law," and "cruel and unusual punishment" jumped out from the pages. Collins continued on with his unsettling chronology.

"The executioner takes the portable electric chair off the truck, and runs an extension cord from the chair into the jail, seeking a source of current. Then prison guards bring out Francis, ask him if he has any last words, secure him to the chair, and cover part of his face with a hood. You will note, class, the sworn statement of the witnesses to this execution, as found at the court's footnote number 2:

Then the electrocutioner turned on the

- 62 -

switch and when he did Willie Francis'
lips puffed out and he groaned and jumped
so that the chair came off the floor.
Apparently the switch was turned on twice
and then the condemned man yelled:
"Take it off. Let me breathe." Affidavit
of official witness Harold Resweber, dated
May 23, 1946.

I saw the electrocutioner turn on the
switch and I saw his lips puff out and
swell, his body tensed and stretched. I
heard the one in charge yell to the man
outside for more juice when he saw that
Willie Francis was not dying and the one
on the outside yelled back he was giving
him all he had. Then Willie Francis
cried out "Take it off. Let me breathe."
Then they took the hood from his eyes
and unstrapped him.

This boy really got a shock when they
turned that machine on. Affidavit of
official witness Ignace Doucet, dated May
30, 1946.

After he was strapped to the chair
the Sheriff of St. Martin Parish asked
him if he had anything to say about
anything and he said nothing. Then the hood
was placed before his eyes. Then the
officials in charge of the electrocution
were adjusting the mechanisms and when the
needle of the meter registered to a certain
point on the dial, the electrocutioner
pulled down on the switch and at the same
time said: 'Goodby Willie.' At that very
moment, Willie Francis' lips puffed out

- 63 -

*and his body squirmed and tensed and he
jumped so that the chair rocked on the
floor. Then the condemned man said
'Take it off. Let me breathe.'
Then the switch was turned off. Then
some of the men left and a few minutes
after the Sheriff of St. Martin Parish,
Mr. E. L. Resweber, came in and
announced that the governor had granted
the condemned man a reprieve. Affidavit
of official chaplain Reverend Maurice L.
Rousseve, dated May 25, 1946.*

Collins looked up from his reading, as if he were a minister at the pulpit.

"An examination of the condemned teenager confirmed that while he had received electrical charges sufficient to burn off his hair and scar his flesh, there was insufficient current to cause death. It was decided to put Francis back in his prison cell, and to call an electrician to fix the defective chair. This unexpected reprieve gave Francis' legal counsel an opportunity to re-evaluate the course of the defendant's fate.

"Was it possible the State of Louisiana's one bite at the apple was all it should get? Could the condemned defendant be twice placed in jeopardy for the same offense, or might a second execution constitute cruel and unusual punishment in violation of the Constitution's equal protection clause of the 14th Amendment?

Collins was formulating question upon question, and not offering a single answer. Thankfully, some other poor soul with a last name at the beginning of the alphabet would be the next sacrificial lamb. I had no answer for the executioner's riddle. Whomever was called upon would need to display a wisdom and foresight far beyond my limited knowledge.

Collins scanned the student roster. I looked down into my textbook, pretending to study, for eye contact, even for a fleeting moment, might prove disastrous.

"Mr. Fox."

Who? What happened to C, D and E? This was all wrong.

"Is there a Mr. Fox here?" the overpowering baritone voice repeated.

An unexpected electrical charge passed through me. Could the rest of the class see my hair standing on end?

"Yes, sir," I blurted out in my best I-want-to-be-a-lawyer voice.

"Mr. Fox, if you were called upon as a Justice of the United States Supreme Court to render a decision in this life and death matter, how would you rule?"

Hundreds of eyeballs bored into me. It was as quiet as the fateful day in fourth grade when I forgot my one and only line in the elementary school play.

Now let's see, if I ruled that Francis should live, Collins would undoubtedly brand me a "bleeding heart softy." If I voted to fry the defendant a second time, I'd need to back it up with some solid reasoning, which had not, at that precise moment, yet entered my swirling brain.

My face was becoming flushed. Would I attempt to formulate a response based on how others might view me. Was not the life of Willie Francis the real issue? Did the Constitution permit a second attempt at execution?

A bell sounded, signaling the end of the first hour of class.

"Mr. Fox," Collins announced. "You, similar to Mr Francis, have gained a brief reprieve. On Wednesday, expect to enlighten the class with your holding in this matter." And with those words, our tutor and provocateur exited the lecture hall, as he had arrived - quickly and without fanfare.

"Good luck, pal," my neighbor to the immediate right offered.

At the conclusion of the day's classes, I entered the law library to research the Willie Francis case chronology. Because of the unusual issues raised by this Supreme Court appeal, several national newspapers had, at the time, actively reported upon developments as the case made its way from the Supreme Court of Louisiana upward to the Supreme Court of the United States. I was fascinated to learn that during the trial, which occurred as World War II was winding down, the alleged murder weapon, a pistol, had been sent to the FBI for analysis. It was "lost in the mail" and was never recovered. Other abnormalities at the trial level were equally suspect. For this reason and several others, some newspapers intimated that the defendant may not have received a fair trial. No appeal from these issues had ever been filed.

The newspapers did carry pictures of both the defendant, and the portable electric chair. Francis looked like some scared kid, peering at the camera through unforgiving prison bars.

I studied the formal Supreme Court opinion, analyzing its esoteric language over and over again. By a scant five to four decision, a majority of five Justices had determined that no legal impropriety had taken place.

"We find nothing here which amounts to cruel and unusual punishment in the constitutional sense," Mr. Justice Reed proclaimed on behalf of the majority. "The fact that the petitioner has already been subjected to a current of electricity does not make his subsequent execution any more cruel than any other execution."

A minority of four Justices disagreed. Mr. Justice Burton wrote on behalf of his brethren Douglas, Murphy, and Rutledge:

> *Electrocution has been approved only in*
> *a form that eliminates suffering.*
> *The Louisiana statute makes this clear.*
> *It provides that:*
> *Every sentence of death imposed in*
> *this State shall be by electrocution; that*
> *is, causing to pass through the body of the*
> *person convicted a current of electricity of*

sufficient intensity to cause death, and the application and continuance of such current through the body of the person convicted until such person is dead. It does not provide for electrocution by interrupted or repeated applications of electric current at intervals of several days or even minutes. It does not provide for the application of electric current of an intensity less than that sufficient to cause death. It prescribes expressly and solely for the application of a current of sufficient intensity to cause death and for the continuance of that application until death results. Prescribing capital punishment, it should be construed strictly. There can be no implied provision for the second, third or multiple application of the current. There is no statutory or judicial precedent upholding a delayed process of electrocution.

I began to wonder. If the five Justices who had decided that Willie Francis should be subjected to a second execution had themselves been strapped into the portable electric chair, would they have been able to draft a convincing argument why a second execution might have been excessive?

Collins appeared promptly at 9 a.m. Wednesday. He had not yet ascended the podium when he called out.

"Mr. Fox, are you present?"

"I am, Professor."

"And have you a reasoned opinion as to whether Willie Francis should die by a second attempted execution?"

"I have an opinion, Professor."

"Very well. Bestow your opinion upon us."

And I did.

CHAPTER SEVEN:
THE NEIGHBORS

Philip and Bonnie Bowser had been searching for their dream home for more than a year with no luck. They were discouraged, drained and losing hope. The realtors kept dragging them from one dump to another. They weren't looking for a miracle, just a cozy Cape Cod on a couple of acres with open space far away from any neighbors. A quaint picture window with a view. A dry basement. A roof that didn't leak. Were these things really too much to ask?

Carlton Windfall, the personable and forever optimistic realtor from "Gettum's Gallery of Finer Homes" just didn't get it. Wasting time was his specialty. He organized tour after tour of unacceptable homes. Dwellings with rat droppings in the kitchen cabinets. Shacks devoid of working plumbing. Lean-tos with crumbling fireplaces located in flood plains. Carlton rationalized each useless showing with this wisdom: "You never know - this could have been the one!"

"Yeah, if 'the one' is an over-priced half-a-double with a leaking toilet and five screaming kids living next door," Philip muttered to himself.

The Bowsers began to fall apart. Loving gestures to one another turned into hurtful words. Mrs. Bowser switched to weekly therapy sessions and upped her dosage of valium. Would they ever leave their luxury garden apartment, a shoebox with neither garden nor luxury? A summer of house searching had turned into fall, and fall into winter.

It was the Tuesday before Christmas, the day after idiotic Carlton had shown them a modular home located down-wind from the city sewage recycling plant. The Bowsers were so despondent, they decided to take a ride out in the country near Heimberg Township. They couldn't stand another minute in that apartment, staring at each other and the artificial Christmas tree, the only type of fireproof decoration the landlord permitted.

As the Bowsers proceeded north along Route 248, there came into view a FiSBO: a property For Sale By Owner. It was a cottage set back from the road with an overstated picture window. The nearest neighbor was 400 feet away. Philip jammed on the brakes. Bonnie gasped. They both knew it. They had found their dream home.

The private driveway was bordered by a newly painted white picket fence. They parked in front of the spacious two-car garage. Silently, their racing eyes drank in the quaint brick and stone Cape Cod. Against their better judgement, they began to bond with its unpretentious, yet inviting, exterior.

"Might as well give it a try," Philip tentatively suggested. The couple alighted from their car, and walked hand-in-hand across the frozen winter lawn to the wooden door with the polished brass kick-plate.

"Honey, this could be it," Bonnie whispered, as she tried to hold back her excitement. Philip rang the doorbell as he admired the matching brass knocker.

Caldwell Teller opened the door, and introduced the giddy couple to his wife, Prudence, who appeared at the kitchen entrance. The aroma of freshly baked chocolate chip cookies filled the air.

The Tellers granted them an impromptu showing. The basement was dry. The roof didn't leak. And the picture window boasted an uninterrupted view of the Blue Mountains. Even more surprising was the price. It was fair and fell well within the Bowser's budgetary constraints.

The couples shook hands on the price and planned to have a written agreement of sale by week's end. As the

Bowsers drove away, they saw Mr. Teller don his winter coat, walk over to the "For Sale" sign and yank it out of the frozen ground.

"Philip," she instructed, "please call the lawyer tomorrow to write up the papers before they change their minds. Promise?"

"I promise," Philip assured her.

The Bowsers appeared at my office the next morning. I prepared the necessary documentation outlining all the terms upon which the parties had concurred, including purchase price, date of settlement, mortgage contingency, home inspection, and list of personal property to remain with the sale. I suggested that the present survey description and the sellers' disclosure statement be attached as exhibits.

"What's that last item you just mentioned?" Mr. Bowser asked.

"It's an affidavit, prepared and signed by the owners, advising you of the present condition of the premises, including the status of heating, plumbing, septic, and water systems. If there are any structural abnormalities or defects, the sellers are required by law to disclose problems that might affect habitability."

Not only did the sellers execute a full disclosure affidavit, but also at my urging, a professional home inspector performed a detailed evaluation, and determined that the residence was in top notch condition.

My clients scheduled settlement for January 30, a bitterly cold day. Temperature aside, all parties appeared at my office on time as requested, and the money, deed, and keys to the front door changed hands without issue. The settlement having concluded, there was only one final topic for me to review with the sellers. I reached for the IRS capital gains reporting form, and addressed Mr. and Mrs. Teller, who had, until that moment, willingly and unhesitatingly complied with the execution of the myriad of documents evidencing the sale of their residence.

"Tell me, folks, to what new address will you be moving?" I inquired.

The pleasant and agreeable smiles that had, during the last hour, highlighted their faces, were replaced by looks of reluctant defensiveness. Moments of uncomfortable silence passed.

"Why do you want to know?" he questioned as he began to rise out of his seat.

"Two reasons," I explained. "The Internal Revenue Service requires that I, as closing agent, advise the government of your future whereabouts, so they can track you down and extract any capital gains taxes that might ultimately be due. Also, after I pay off your mortgage, there may be a refund, and I am required to send those monies to you."

The sellers weren't convinced. They looked at each other, then at me. As Mr. Teller helped his wife with her coat, they spoke simultaneously:

"We're heading out West," Mr. Teller announced.

"We're going South," Mrs. Teller contradicted.

"What we mean to say," Mr. Teller continued, "is that we're retiring and plan to travel. A lot."

"Well, that sounds wonderful," I remarked, "but I need a formal address where you will be receiving your mail in the future."

"Well ... " Mr. Teller hesitated as he fiddled with his gloves and found his keys, "use ... use our daughter's address over in Phillipsburg, New Jersey. It's 121 North Highland Street."

I printed the suspect data on the IRS form. The settlement having ended, everyone stood up and shook hands. Mr. Teller quickly placed the proceeds check in his wallet, nodded to his wife, and they left my office without so much as another word.

- - - - - - - - - - - - - - - - - - -

I can't recall ever suffering through such a brutal winter. The outside temperature during January and February never reached above 20 degrees. Finally, though, spring arrived, and with it the robin redbreasts and the milder temperatures. People began to venture outdoors again, and in Florida, a new season of major league baseball had begun.

Upon arriving at my office, I looked through the morning mail and prepared for my first appointment. That's when I noticed that my secretary, Cathy, had added another client consultation to my schedule for 3:30 in the afternoon - Mr. and Mrs. Bowser. I called out to her.

"Are those the nice folks who bought that brick Cape a couple months back?"

"Yes," Cathy confirmed from the next room.

"Is there a problem?"

"I asked, but they said it was too complicated to get into over the phone."

Rats! I hate surprises. If the problem was outside my area of expertise, the session would be a waste of time for everyone. Cathy noted my concern.

"They assured me you could take care of it."

"Maybe you better find their settlement file," I said. "There could be some question about their new home."

The Bowsers arrived on time to the minute and were ushered into the same conference room where a mere four months ago they had purchased their dream home.

"It's a pleasure to see you again," I began as we shook hands. Then I stepped in it. "How's the new house?"

"Oh my God," Mr. Bowser said.

"We don't even know where to begin," Mrs. Bowser cut in. "See, the neighbors down the street are serial killers. They're burying their victims in their backyard. Can't you do something?"

That's what I like about the practice of law - fresh and exciting problems present themselves every day, like a sunflower bud bursting into bloom.

"You see," Mrs. Bowser added, "this winter we kept the house sealed up like a piece of Tupperware because of the harsh cold, so we never smelled the decomposing bodies."

"And they weren't burying as many victims anyway

'cause the ground was frozen," Mr. Bowser added.

"But now it's springtime," Mrs. Bowser said, "and there are 30 or 40 fresh shallow graves. They're murdering more people each week. The stench is overwhelming. We can't open our windows."

I'm generally inclined not to interrupt a client's narrative, but a few questions came to mind.

"How do you know they are murdering people?"

"Their house is only about four hundred feet away," Mrs. Bowser explained. After we began to smell the problem, we decided to investigate. One night, we crept over to their house, and peeked through the backyard fence. That's when we first saw it in the glow of the moonlight - about a hundred shallow graves! All windows of the house had heavy drawn curtains, but we could still hear blood-curdling screams coming from within. People inside were being tortured and killed."

"And then we noticed that every Tuesday, just before midnight, they'd conduct a candlelight procession out to the backyard cemetery to bury the dead," Mr. Bowser added. "It's always the same three creepy pallbearers, and always dressed in black. It's the only time we see them, except when they drive a car loaded with bodies into their garage, but that only takes a second, since their garage door opener is pretty fast."

"We just know the Tellers knew the neighbors were mass murderers and that's why they unloaded the house at a modest price. They didn't want to get involved," Mrs. Bowser theorized. "Anyway, shouldn't they have disclosed all this? I mean, if we had known about the deaths, we would have passed on the house, or at least negotiated a better price."

An interesting question. The sellers' disclosure form focused solely upon the condition of the real estate being purchased. It didn't require disclosure of any psychopathic actions attributable to the neighbors.

How much had Mr. and Mrs. Teller known that they weren't telling? Is this why they moved away? As I paged through the file, I noted that a letter I had sent to them after settlement, enclosing a small utility rebate payment, had been returned indicating "no such address" on the envelope. While my clients were present, I checked the forwarding address the sellers had given me with a current map of Phillipsburg. There was no North Highland Street.

"You don't believe us," Mrs. Bowser said flatly. "I know ... why not come over this Tuesday night for the next death march. If the wind is right, you'll be able to hear the screams clear as a bell."

I was trapped. If I contacted the police, and this story turned out to be the obvious hoax I knew it was, the cops might petition to have my competency reviewed. If I ignored the Bowsers, there was one chance in a million I could have stopped the torture and disposal of scores of innocent victims. I agreed to meet the Bowsers at the crime scene on Tuesday night. That would give me enough time to go to the courthouse and research the tax assessment records to determine just who in heaven's name owned the ill-begotten residence next door.

The following day's journey to the courthouse raised more questions than it answered. My review of the county tax assessment records uncovered the disquieting fact that the property bordering that of my clients was not owned by anyone in particular. Rather, the deed was held in the name of the "Blankenhorn Trust," and the trustee overseeing it was designated as "The Farmers Home Bank of Cleveland." This unorthodox form of residential land ownership caught my attention. So I copied the deed, the tax records, and the assessment map, all of which only confirmed that the neighbors' macabre house, known as 2318 Heimberg Road, was situated on a rectangular parcel of land approximately four acres in area. The present deed of record referenced the fact that the prior owner, Nathan Blankenhorn, widower, had departed this life about 30 years ago, whereupon his estate had transferred title to the land into the name of the bank as trustee.

I then researched Blankenhorn's estate file at the

county Register of Wills office. The decedent had died testate, his holographic last will and testament acknowledging the existence of three emancipated daughters. Blankenhorn had, in his own hand, penned an inarticulately drafted trust, providing for his daughters, and had named the bank now serving as trustee. I decided that a call to that bank might place events in their correct perspective, and would further serve to dispel the ridiculous thoughts entertained by Mr. and Mrs. Bowser.

Almost every bank in Pennsylvania seems to have merged, consolidated, or otherwise changed its name more often than the Federal Reserve tampers with interest rates. This was not true of The Farmers Home Bank of Cleveland, Ohio. This financial institution still maintained its one and only name and office at the same location where Nathan Blankenhorn had first found it. I had gathered enough information. It was time to call the trustee.

"Good morning. Farmers Home Bank. How may I help you?"

It was the pleasant helpful voice of a live young lady, not some "press one - press two" recording. Perhaps customer service was not dead after all.

"Hello, this is Larry Fox. Does your institution maintain a trust department?"

"Yes. Allow me to transfer you to Mr. J. S. Pinkerton. One moment, please. And thank you for calling."

So very efficient. For a moment, I thought about transferring my deposits to Cleveland.

"Pinkerton here. What can I do for you?"

"Hello, this is Larry Fox. I'm an attorney in Bethlehem, Pennsylvania."

Pinkerton was unimpressed. "Yes?"

On second thought, the service in Ohio wasn't much better than in Pennsylvania. I decided to leave my deposits where they were.

"I'm calling regarding the Nathan Blankenhorn Trust. Does that name sound familiar?"

There was dead silence on the other end of the phone,

but that was to be expected - this was a trust department.

"Yes," came the hesitant response. "What is your interest in the trust, Mr. Fox?"

"I represent Philip and Bonnie Bowser, clients who reside next door to 2318 Heimberg Road in Lehigh County, Pennsylvania and - "

"And they believe mass murder is taking place at the Blankenhorn house?" Pinkerton interrupted.

Now I was dead silent. "How did you know?" I stammered.

"A few months back I received several irritating calls from somebody named Caldwell Teller. He related some idiotic tale about torture, and screaming, and burials in a make-shift cemetery. Quite frankly, you folks in Pennsylvania could use a good hobby shop. Too much time on your hands."

Those stinkin' Tellers. They knew about the death chambers and mayhem, and conveniently left it off the sellers' disclosure form. Then, they went into hiding.

"Mr. Pinkerton," I resumed, "did you ever bother to investigate the allegations?"

"No. It's not my job. Have you? Listen, I just pay the bills received by the trust. If you have lingering concerns about mass murder or, whatever, perhaps you and yours should contact the proper authorities."

"But have you personally visited the house that you administer?" I pressed.

Click. He was gone.

A sense of disquieting panic washed over me. If both the Tellers and the Bowsers had independently reached the same conclusion, was it possible that the unspeakable was... But then, calm reflection began to prevail. After all, my job was to certify that the Bowsers received clear title to their property. If an illegal torture chamber or unlicensed cemetery existed next door, that was the Blankenhorn Trust's problem, or that of the township zoning officer. Moreover, by Tuesday night, after I had taken a look for myself, all this nonsense would surely come to an end.

The ride to Heimberg Township was uneventful. Even though it was a dark, moonless night, I had no trouble locating the Bowser residence. I arrived at about 11:00 o'clock, well in time for any impromptu midnight funeral processions.

Despite the late hour, the Bowsers were expecting me, and greeted me as I approached the front door. The porch light disclosed an idyllic and well-maintained country cottage, secure from the noise and confusion of the overpopulated city.

I stood outside, momentarily sniffing the mild evening air, in an attempt to detect any unusual odors. Mr. Bowser picked up on my experiment.

"Tonight's is a westerly wind, toward the mass graves, so you won't smell much until we get closer," he explained. "But first, why don't you come on in, have some fresh-baked banana bread and take a tour of our little house. They probably won't start digging and chanting for another hour or so."

"Who chants?" I asked as I stepped inside.

"The pallbearers," Mrs. Bowser clarified. "There are three of them and they drape themselves in black cloth. If it weren't for the candles they carry, we wouldn't even know that much."

"That's right," Mr. Bowser continued. "There aren't any street lights around here, and their backyard is as dark as the inside of a cow. But by tomorrow morning, we'll see more new shallow graves."

"Coffee?" Mrs. Bowser offered.

If the Bowsers were insane, I had yet to see it. Their home was cozy, they were rather congenial, and the banana bread could have won first prize at the Great Allentown Fair. We sat by the large picture window and made small talk until about 11:30. That's when a car with darkened headlights made its way slowly up the neighbor's driveway. It disappeared behind the obedient automatic garage door.

I spilled my coffee. Something was definitely amiss here. Suddenly, I wasn't so confident the Bowsers were telling tall tales. It was time to call the police.

"The cops!" Mrs. Bowser laughed out loud. "This is Heimberg Township. There isn't a police department within a 30-mile radius. The nearest state police barracks is down in Limeport. You call them now and they might be here - by tomorrow."

She might be right, but better late than never, I thought. I began to think of excuses why a sudden emergency back in Bethlehem required my immediate attention. Hesitation was written on my face. They both looked at me as if I were the cowardly lion, fearful of asking the Wizard of Oz for some courage.

"Is anything wrong?" Mrs. Bowser inquired intently.

Well, what the hell - it couldn't hurt to peek over the neighbor's backyard fence just for a second.

We crept outside on tip-toe. Mrs. Bowser served as head scout. Soon, we had approached enemy territory. A repulsive odor slapped my face. I was about to lose the coffee and banana bread, but Mr. Bowser signaled to remain still. We raised our collective eyes to the top of the fence. The Bowsers sustained themselves on just half breaths. I stopped breathing altogether.

Three dark shrouded images, each holding but a single candle to illuminate their path, carried a long narrow box as they chanted something unintelligible into the night air. They marched solemnly toward three shovels that leaned upright upon one another, placed in sacred position venerating an unknown god. Chunks of dirt flew in the air as they dug yet another grave. Progress was deliberate, but slow, suggesting that these nocturnal laborers were hindered by some concealed infirmity. Yet, they patiently remained committed to their excavation. One would mumble as another would acquiesce. Plotting, tending, digging - all with a significance known only to them.

A forsaken aura belied their darkened residence.

Still, it was the demonic, yet muted, wailing - an unmistakable inhuman multitude of pleas for help that intermittently escaped the confines within - that grasped my soul.

I had seen and heard enough. I was about to turn away when Mr. Bowser pointed to the trilogy of grave diggers. The evil three lowered their latest victim into the ground and heaped a blanket of fresh earth over top, leaving yet another naked mound of dirt, similar to the scores of others barely visible in the blackness of night. We crept back to our camp in silence.

I called the authorities at once. The next day bright and early at 10:30 a.m. the Limeport State Police assigned 24-year old Corporal Adams to investigate.

The 6-foot 2-inch strapping officer drove his patrol car up the mysterious driveway to the dilapidated house whose front porch was accentuated with a rotting claw-foot velour covered sofa. Threads and forgotten spider webs tangled together. Dead plants rotted in broken clay pots positioned at each end of the sofa. One of the containers had sunk into a broken floorboard. A lone arthritic cat ambled away, puzzled by the sight of a visitor. Hanging from ripped window coverings was a brown wreath sporting a hand-painted plaque that read "Welcome To Our Home."

The officer knocked on the unpainted door. No answer. And from within issued forth torturous wailing and the smell of death. Corporal Adams tentatively stepped around the broken floorboards and next surveyed the backyard grave sites. He called immediately for back-up and a SWAT team.

Within a half hour, the crime scene was surrounded by helmeted police officers wearing flak jackets. A helicopter hovered overhead. Lieutenant Bigbees and his bull horn took charge.

"THROW DOWN YOUR WEAPONS AND EXIT THE RESIDENCE WITH YOUR HANDS CLASPED BEHIND YOUR HEAD," Bigbees hollered to the unseen enemy from his vantage point inside the bulletproof SWAT van. Nothing happened. The 30-odd grim-faced officers encircling the site aimed their automatic weapons and stood fast.

"THIS IS YOUR LAST CHANCE BEFORE WE BREAK DOWN THE DOOR AND IMPLODE THE WINDOWS," Bigbees blared. Again, nothing.

The lieutenant gave his secret SWAT signal to the door- breaking specialist in preparation for destruction of the entranceway. Corporal Muvinsky dutifully lifted his ramrod device from the back of the bulletproof SWAT van and fearlessly made his way to the front porch - 30 automatic weapons at their ready behind him.

Then it happened. With but two seconds before impact, someone from within inched open the unpainted and splintered door. Muvinsky was the only one who could hear the pitiful, fragile voice.

"If I open it any more, the cats will get out."

Muvinsky had been trained for any possible form of subterfuge, and as a result, had advanced within his department to "door-basher" status. But here, he simply pushed the door open with his index finger, then swiftly handcuffed octogenarian, Matilda Blankenhorn.

And then it started. At first, there were just 20 or 30 of them. But moments later, another 40 or 50 cats escaped out the front door. Scores of police officers ran toward the house. The cops wanted in. The cats wanted out. Both groups did as they pleased with little concern for the other party scampering past in the opposite direction.

Soon the police had located two other human occupants, Elsie and Mabel Blankenhorn, both of whom appeared to be close to 90 years of age. They, too, were handcuffed and led out as some of the slower geriatric cats hobbled along side them through the open door. Police estimated about 250 felines had escaped. Many others, the infirm and the sick, lay about in every room of the house. The smell defied description.

With time, the police and social workers from the County Department of Aging uncovered enough facts for the court which in turn determined that guardians should be appointed to administer the affairs of the three spinster sisters. Apparently, Matilda, Elsie, and Mabel had lived at the old homestead their entire lives. Their father had, on occasion, acknowledged that his girls were a little "off," and so he named his brother, a banker at The Farmers Home Bank, as trustee of the funds accumulated at time of his death. Ultimately, the brother died, too, at which point the bank's trust department assumed administration of the trust. When the daughters needed money, they simply contacted the bank for a check.

As years passed, the sisters' love for cats had apparently turned to obsession and their collective mental health deteriorated. They became nocturnal in their habits, similar to the stray cats they sought to "rescue" during their nighttime forays in the ancient Studebaker that had last undergone a state vehicle inspection 20 years earlier. Only Elsie was physically able to drive, but the other two sisters did their part by luring unsuspecting cats into large cloth bags.

About midnight, they would return with the evening's catch and add them to the growing collection of howling prisoners. The money sent from the bank was used for cat food. Once a week, on Tuesdays, those cats that had died were buried in the backyard during solemn funeral services. Over the years, scores of cats had found their final resting place there.

The court also ruled that Pinkerton and his bank had failed to adequately oversee the welfare of the sisters, and the judge wisely removed them as trustees. The three ladies were ultimately lodged together at a quaint rest home that agreed to let them keep one cat. The Department of Health successfully petitioned to raze the old homestead. The Department of Environmental Protection requisitioned some of the trust funds in order to unearth and remove the more than 1,000 grave sites.

And the Bowsers? Two years later, Mr. Bowser received a transfer to the West Coast, and so they had to sell their dream home after all. They asked me to represent them in the sale of the residence to a nice young couple who had fallen in love with the place the minute they saw the "For Sale By Owner" sign.

I prepared a "Sellers' Disclosure Statement" for signature by the Bowsers. They affirmed that the cottage was in "mint condition," but they included one caveat: sometimes ghosts could be seen at work after midnight in the field next door, and wailing sounds often kept the Bowsers up at night in the springtime.

The new purchasers giggled at the preposterous warning.

CHAPTER EIGHT:
BETTER SAFE THAN SORRY

My office building was constructed well over a century ago. Many have mistakenly assumed that its design is Victorian. In truth, this former private mansion stands as one of Bethlehem's finest examples of Georgian design. This proud structure was created by skilled artisans, none of whom used a single piece of power equipment or computer-generated blueprints. Similar to the builders of the pyramids, these folks obviously knew what they were doing, and took pride in their work. The Greek columns supporting the front portico, designed with an entasis, are complimented by massive red brick and stone walls, in which are situated sunken windows through which a grand piano could pass. Each window boasts an exterior arch comprised of tan bricks supported at the apex by a hand-cut cornerstone.

It could be argued that the crowning achievement of their labors consists of the first floor circular walnut stairway, bordered by delicate hand-carved cherry spindles and banister. But I would disagree. Each morning, as I enter the tile vestibule, I never cease to marvel at the 7-foot exterior oak door and the accompanying interior mosaic glass that stand as silent guards to the reception area. The outside door is complimented by a custom-designed brass doorknob plate that is more than one foot in length. The exterior door possesses a 4-foot by 3-foot lead crystal hand-rolled one-inch thick pane of glass with three concentric parallel beveled borders, intentionally designed to catch and disburse the sun's rays.

The interior vestibule door, adorned with overhead transom, is artistically unique. It is composed of hundreds of symmetrically cut crystal pieces that create an intricate pattern between fine curved walnut strands that comprise this one-of-a-kind entranceway. There may not exist today anyone capable of reconstructing such a masterpiece.

- -

The certified letter from the Pennsylvania Department of Labor and Industry arrived without warning. At first, I thought that perhaps a client had run afoul of some state building code regulation. But as I read the missive, it became clear that I was the object of the Commonwealth's concern.

> *Dear Sir:*
> *Our recent on-site inspection of your offices disclosed that the front entranceway doors consist in part of flammable materials in violation of Article 7, Section 110.18(b) of the state fire and safety code. Please submit proof of compliance within 30 days of the above date.*
>
> *Very truly yours,*
> *Inspections Department*

I called the Department of Labor and Industry. Mr. Ferguson took the call.

"That's right, Mr. Fox. Our records indicate that you converted a private residence into a structure now accessed by the public, yet there are no metal fire and panic doors. Wood is unacceptable."

"The doors have been there for over a century. This is an historic building. The entranceway is irreplaceable."

"Come, come, Mr. Fox - here at L & I, we have found that anything can be replaced. And remember you can always paint a metal door to look just like wood. No one will ever know the difference."

It was at this point in the conversation that I asked Mr. Ferguson how I might pursue an appeal from his initial determination. He scheduled a formal hearing for the next month before the Labor and Industry Appeals Board. It convened in Harrisburg.

I decided I better leave nothing to chance. I took color photographs of each side of both doors. I retained an architect who certified in writing that the craftsmanship was historically significant, and that replacement of the doors would irreparably damage the artistic integrity of the building. Then, on the appointed day, I drove 87 miles to Harrisburg, the capital of the Commonwealth of Pennsylvania.

It took some doing, but I located the Department of Labor and Industry Offices. They were hidden in a massive square structure. Several large first floor metal fire and panic doors granted ingress to the public. There wasn't a piece of cut lead crystal to be found anywhere. I took the elevator up to the fourth floor, and soon became a spectator to the first appeal hearing of the day.

A Mr. McIlerney had just taken the witness stand, and now sat facing the three administrative referees. I joined seven other condemned souls in the audience. Apparently each of us had one thing in common: We were outlaws.

But Mr. McIlerney was in deeper than I. One of his employees had, while backing up a truck, accidentally poured three cubic yards of cement on another employee. Poor Harry Johnson had nearly become a pre-cast mummy similar to the ancient victims of Pompeii during the eruption of Mount Vesuvius. McIlerney, however, didn't think his company should have been cited for a safety violation, since he claimed there had been compliance with not just one, but two separate safety requirements.

"Look," he explained to the trilogy of judges, "I admit, as Stan was backing up the truck, he did pour a load of concrete on Harry ... "

"Did your truck have an audible beeping signal as it moved in reverse?" one judge asked.

"Of course," McIlerney confirmed.

"Then please explain how Mr. Johnson was unaware of the truck alarm?" the second judge inquired.

"Because the law also requires that all my employees wear ear protectors. Harry never heard the damn truck approaching," McIlerney explained.

The conflicting laws confused the judges, who decided they would take the case "under advisement" - the legal term for "we'll never be able to make a decision on this one."

- - - - - - - - - - - - - -

It was the summer after my freshman year in college - a time when Bethlehem Steel Corporation was still pouring molten rivers of red hot metal on the south side of the city after which it took its name. More than 16,000 men and women worked around the clock on three separate shifts for this steel producing conglomerate known around the world. This giant was so big, it operated its own railroad within the confines of the local plant, the *P B N E*, or *Philadelphia, Bethlehem, and New England* line. Some skeptics thought it stood for Poor Bonus and No Earnings.

The day after school ended, I joined 75 other students hired that same week. We all showed up Monday morning at the "Main Gate" and were bused two miles behind the imposing metal fences that separated steel workers from the rest of the world.

Inside, the indoctrination center smelled like a hospital. It was a hospital. Of sorts. The next eight hours brought physical examinations and psychological evaluations. In addition, a mountain of safety equipment was heaped on me, including an identification badge, a hard hat, metatarsal shoes, ear protectors, eyeglass side-shields, gloves, and even a heavy-duty jockstrap. Nothing, it seemed, went unprotected at "the Steel." Our assignments came next. Some of us went to the soaking pits; others to the beam yards, the forge, or the ingot mold. I'd never see any of these new hires again. After all, the plant was huge. It rambled on for more than six miles along the Lehigh River.

Seven other newbies and I drew duty at the iron foundry.

"The foundry? What's that?" the kid next to me asked.

I shrugged my shoulders, grabbed my safety equipment, and got back on the bus. It was 4:00 o'clock and we drove on for yet another mile, past grimy blast furnaces and towering coke ovens.

"Gate Four," the bus driver hollered. He handed us our work schedules for the next two weeks. I was to report the next night at 11:00 o'clock.

"Be here by 10:30," he said. "That'll give you time to get a locker and get changed." The bus ultimately returned us to the main gate. Our day of indoctrination had ended.

This would be my life until the fall. A laborer on the graveyard shift in the iron foundry. I was an official steel worker, like my father and grandfather before him.

A day passed by quickly and before I knew it, I was back at Gate Four at 10:30 p.m. I was already lost. Things looked mighty different in the dark. I approached the nearest security guard.

"Could you point me in the direction of the iron foundry?" I asked. The guard smirked.

"You see all them lights way over there to the left, and to the right ...?"

"Yes ... "

"And the big dark area in the middle ...?"

"Yes ... "

"That's the foundry."

I stumbled along, tripping over chunks of slag scattered in the roadway. A dark figure soon joined me from behind, for he apparently knew how to walk without hesitation on the discarded by-product.

"Could you tell me where the door is?" I asked.

"Door? Ain't no doors in a foundry, kid. Just heat and fumes. You better follow me."

My impromptu guide and I journeyed through a long hallway illuminated by one 40-watt bulb.

"It's so dark," I offered.

"Yeah, well this ain't Atlantic City, friend. And there ain't no Miss America Pageant here this week."

We stopped at a dented, rusty box hung on a pole. I watched as he reached for his card, and punched the clock.

"This your first day?"

"Yes, sir."

"Don't 'sir' me. I ain't no foreman. Find your card, and punch it."

I did as instructed. Next we entered a cavernous room illuminated by three or four forlorn bulbs. It was four times brighter than the hallway and like everything else around me, it had no doors. No doors, but damn if it didn't have 40 toilets lined up in a row similar to an army boot camp setting. Three men, all wearing hard hats and seated intermittently upon select porcelain thrones in the eerie light, read newspapers or betting sheets they had found abandoned on the floor. There were 40 showers on the other side. A few more employees were using those.

My guide had vanished, but the void was about to be filled.

"You a new hire?" a short toothless bald man inquired.

I could only stare as I realized I was a participant in a nightmare come true.

"I'm the janitor. You'll need a locker for your stuff. Follow me."

We walked past two guys in position on the toilets.

"Hiya, Pappy," one called out to my new janitor friend.

The other fellow, engaged in mid-bowel movement, made small talk about the demise of the Phillies.

What the hell was wrong with these people? Just then I made a silent promise. Never would I sink to group toileting.

Pappy escorted me into yet another sprawling room.

Oddly enough, it too, had no door. There stood row upon row of backless wooden benches, resting on metal "I" beam supports.

"This is for your locker," Pappy advised as he handed me a small brass key upon which was imprinted four numbers.

I turned 360 degrees, and then back again, yet saw no lockers. Then I glanced upward. Like a scene similar to one of the descending levels in *Dante's Inferno*, hundreds upon hundreds of boots dangled above me. It was as if the souls of the shoes of the damned had been left to hang forever in this doorless wilderness.

Pappy pointed to a wall. There, to my amazement, were hundreds of metal chains rising skyward connected to the countless hanging boots. Pappy led me to my chain. On it was a lock. I held the key.

"When you open the lock, slowly let the chain run through your hand, so no one gets belted by a run-a-way basket."

Basket? What basket? It didn't matter. I did as commanded. I opened the lock. The chain moved upward. Simultaneously, a wire metal basket dangling 100 feet skyward, descended from the ceiling, coming to rest an inch from my nose.

"There's your locker, kid," Pappy announced.

All those hundreds of shoes were tied to the bottom of countless baskets. Other personal property, like shower shoes, soap, and safety equipment, was stored inside.

"Your shift starts in 15 minutes. Get dressed and report through that passageway to the left," Pappy advised through his barren upper and lower gums. Then he was gone - off to clean the toilets. This would be a job similar to painting the Golden Gate Bridge. He would never be quite finished.

Safety shoes. Gloves. Hard hat. Ear protectors. No problem. The eyeglass side-shields? That was different. If I put one shield on the left side of my glasses, the right refused to fit, and vice versa. The only way they both worked properly was if the left one stuck into my left eye socket, while the right simultaneously rubbed against my right temple. Such a tormenting configuration would, under Labor and Industry standards, ensure my safety.

With just 10 minutes before my shift was to begin, I rushed to lace up my 5-pound metatarsal safety shoes. It was at this frenzied moment that I realized I had forgotten to install the company-issued blue plastic jockstrap. Damn! What if they conducted an emergency jockstrap inspection and I came up wanting. Would they fire me for not supporting company policy? With just eight minutes left, there was no time to lose. I'd have to unlace my safety shoes, take off my pants, and position the jock- strap with the strange little white elastic belt around my fanny.

Finished. I, along with my 5-pound shoes, the uncomfortable jockstrap, sweaty hard hat, eye-poking side-shields, oversized ear protectors, and leather gloves designed to fit Godzilla, waddled into the foreboding hallway leading to the foundry.

I can remember as a youngster visiting Niagara Falls with my family. As we drove to within 3 miles of the attraction, I began to hear what would ultimately become a constant bone-rattling thunder. And so it was with the iron foundry - a place so loud it was impossible to engage in even simple conversation.

I entered the dark abyss, joining other condemned prisoners of the graveyard shift as they shuffled along like lifeless robots. Any joy in this place was found only on the sooty faces of those who had ended their shifts and were now passing us in the opposite direction. These animated souls stepped smartly toward the locker room despite the weight of their metatarsal shoes.

All around, everyone seemed to have a place and reason for being in the foundry, except me. I stood at an entranceway big enough for a locomotive to pass through. Indeed, railroad tracks crisscrossed the worn cement floor.

"You a new hire?" a voice from under a green safety hat inquired.

"Yes, sir."

I would soon come to learn that green hats were worn by supervisory foremen, white by plant executives, yellow by hourly workers, and yellow hats decorated with large red safety stripes by neophytes like me.

"Where's your respirator?"

"My what?"

"Your blue plastic respirator. You know, it fits over your mouth and nose?"

No wonder my jockstrap was already beginning to chafe at the edges.

"The respirator ..." I stammered. "I thought it was a ... that is ... I must have left it in my locker ... I mean my basket."

"Well, don't just stand there. Go get it. Meet me back here in five minutes," the foreman scolded above the din of steam whistles and screeching overhead cranes.

I was back. The foreman and I then walked a distance of a city block, the whirl of machinery and commotion of men laboring all around us. Mr. Green Hat had one goal in mind. We soon stood before a sign the size of a dump truck. It was suspended on a faded brick wall, perhaps 15 feet above floor level. Its message was simple:

361 Days Without An Injury

Safety Is No Accident

"Kid?"

"Yes ... "

"See that?"

"Yes ... "

"We ain't had no injuries for three hundirt sixty-one days. If we don't have none for one straight year, do you know what happens?"

"No sir."

"Every man in here, all 670 of us, gets a day off with pay. In my 28 years, it's never happened. Know why?

Some shithead always falls into a pit and melts himself into an ingot and ruins things for the rest of us. Not this year. Do I make myself clear?"

"Um, yes sir."

"If you injure yourself in the next four days, and survive, I'll kill you. Is *that* clear?"

"Yes."

"Good. Now that we've had our little chat, we can get to work." The green hat bent down and effortlessly located a steel reinforcement bar on the dented concrete floor. The round quarter-inch bar measured about one and a half feet in length. "This here is a re-bar. Wherever you walk, you'll find 'em. Your job is to take that wheelbarrow over there and pick up every re-bar you find, and dump 'em. Got it?"

"Yes sir."

There were a gazillion re-bars - everywhere. Where had they come from? What was their purpose? How long had they littered the foundry floor?

I grabbed my wheelbarrow and began to graze for re-bars. Each time I stooped to pick one up, my hard hat would slide down over my glasses, causing the safety side-shields to dig into my eye sockets. But I was thankful for the ability to bend at the waist, now that I was using the jockstrap as a respirator.

This hard hat is useless, I mused. Hell, if a steel beam falls on me, I'm dead anyway.

Just then, an overhead craneman lifting a load of steel appeared. He labored between the ceiling beams more than 100 feet above me, but his years of experience had graced him with flawless accuracy. As he flew among the beams, he let loose a mouthful of chewing tobacco that effortlessly found its mark in the middle of the red cross on the top of my hard hat. Never again did I question its usefulness.

My wheelbarrow was now full of re-bars. I sought the advice of the first green hat I could find. Conversation amidst the mayhem of the foundry was impossible. I instinctively pointed at my wheelbarrow, and the foreman nodded his head in affirmation. Raising his hand above his helmet, he made a short circular motion. Soon, an overhead crane appeared from out of nowhere, and a large metal chain descended to within mere inches of my pile of scrap metal.

The foreman produced an iron hand-held hook, and deftly lassoed the wheelbarrow with the 100-pound chain, similar to a cowboy roping a calf. The supervisor completed another circular motion of his hand. Then, before my astonished eyes, the wheelbarrow and its cargo vanished upward into the rarefied atmosphere of the foundry rafters. The crane slithered away in a trail of sparks, carrying its new cargo across the length of the entire foundry to a waiting open railroad boxcar. With one experienced motion, the crane operator lowered the wheelbarrow into the train, dumped the cargo, yet maintained possession of the wheelbarrow, which was then raised and transported across the roof of the foundry back to its original location next to me. The entire operation had taken less than a minute.

I was beginning to see that the men laboring in this inferno were master craftsmen who knew their trade well. Soon I, too, would utilize the time-tested hand signals that served in part as universal steel language.

My first day as a steelworker ended at 7:00 a.m. As a result of my labors, there were several hundred fewer re-bars scattered about the floor. I felt I had accomplished something, certainly, for I was tired, dirty, and sore.

Scores of exhausted men filed toward the locker room, as the day shift of expressionless replacements shuffled past us in the opposite direction.

Some men in the shower room mentioned a place called *Gerts* - a bar two blocks away at Third and Filbert Streets. This watering hole opened at 7:30 a.m. every day to serve the needs of the graveyard shift. Men had been enjoying shot and beer breakfasts there for 30 years. No one could actually recall "Gert," who had died years before. One of the cranemen turned to me.

"You coming, scooter pie?"

"Who, me?"

"Yeah, you. You look like you could use a boilermaker."

"A what?"

"A shot and a beer. It makes it easier to face the old lady."

"Old lady? I'm only 18."

"I don't give a rat's ass how old you are. I'm simply sayin' you could use a belt or two."

I was about to respond, when a guy passed between us on his way to the shower. Except for his noisy wooden shower clogs, the man was naked, a fact of little significance, since most everyone there was in some stage of undress. Nonetheless, he had a tattoo of a rattlesnake's rattle just below his chin. The rest of the reptile's image projected downward about five inches onto his upper chest. At that point, the snake's body, depicted in green, wrapped three times around the man's upper torso, with the head of the snake, jaws wide open, ending at a place I probably would have tried to cover with my respirator.

"Hey Snaky!"

"Yeah?"

"Goin' to Gert's?"

"Yeah. Save my stool."

Who the hell would have dared take it? I soon learned that most everyone had a nickname. It was clear how Snaky got his. And while not everyone was designated as a species within the animal kingdom, I would, in time, be referred to simply as *Foxy*.

By the second evening, I tried my best to look, walk, and talk like a steelworker. I also began to decipher the rather complex code of behavior and conduct expected within this substratum of society.

My first lesson, *Thou shalt not take another's sustenance* would come during the 3:00 a.m. lunch break. About 40 men made their way to an old dented upright refrigerator located next to the foundry furnace. While some workers used safety hand-hooks to cook impaled hot dogs over a molten beam of steel, others began to sit on wooden benches and eat from their lunch boxes.

A guy named Pickles opened the refrigerator, grabbed his bottle of tomato juice, and studied the level of its contents with a suspicious eye. Then turning to the others, he bellowed above the incessant foundry noise, "Who the hell drank my juice?"

Of the 40 men present, not one spoke up.

"Well, I thought this might happen again," he said, "so last night I pissed in the bottle just for kicks."

Just then, the brute sitting next to me shot up to his feet and looked about in disbelief. Within seconds he was buckled over and disgorging his lunch. A valuable lesson had been learned by all. By the next week, food theft complaints had dropped to an all-time low.

Lunch was over, so I located my wheelbarrow, and began collecting re-bars again. An aged foreman counting the days until his retirement was lumbering toward the illuminated sign that silently declared the number of record-setting injury-free days. A red number "4" the size of a car radiator dangled in his gloved hand. He looked at the stairway as if it were Mount Everest. Then he spied me coming toward him. He squinted through his safety glasses at the nickname painted on my hard hat.

"Hey, Foxy ... "

"Yes, sir ... "

"See them numbers up there?"

"Yes, sir ... "

"Do me a favor, will ya? Go up there and put this here number 4 where the 3 is. Got it?"

"Yes, sir." I set down my wheelbarrow, and took the oversized number from the wheezing green hat. The journey up the stairs was uneventful, and I successfully switched the numbers. It was official. The foundry personnel had been injury-free for 364 days. I turned to descend back to floor level.

And then it happened. I think it was the protective steel toe of my metatarsal work boot that first became wedged in the no-slip corrugated surface of the safety stairs.

Within moments, I began to careen downward, so I instinctively grabbed for the bright yellow safety handrail. Unfortunately my heavy-duty safety gloves, one still clutching the record-breaking number 3, were too large to grip anything. My OSHA-stamped hard hat fell over my eyes. My regulation goggles smashed onto the bridge of my nose, as the side-shields dug into my eyes, all of which dislodged my safety respirator, which then jammed into my mouth.

If only I had worn that damn respirator as a jockstrap, I thought to myself, as my safety ear protectors unsnapped and slid sideways across my face. The last thing I remember was falling head over heels bouncing down step-by-step, not missing a single one.

When I regained consciousness, I found myself supine under a crowd of concerned faces. There were a few green hats, including the wheezing numbers guy, Pickles, and two cranemen. Beyond them, I saw stars - not the cartoon type. Rather, these were the real heavenly bodies of our solar system. Indeed, I was staring up at the early morning sky.

"Where am I?" I asked everyone.

"Near Gate 4," Pickles said. "We dragged your sorry ass out here on the Q.T. We figured if you were merely injured, we could throw your body into the parking lot, and drive over it a couple of times until you were dead. If you're OK, though, we'll be happy to walk you back to the foundry."

It was nice to be surrounded by concerned co-workers. I finally stood up and gave the green hat the number 3 I was still clutching. Then we all walked back to the foundry where the safety record remained unblemished. The next day, everyone received a day off with pay. I needed it - to recover from the scrapes and bruises I had sustained while being dragged unconscious out of the foundry.

- - - - - - - - - - - - - - - - - -

The three Labor and Industry judges, having concluded their recess, filed back into the courtroom. I stopped dreaming about steel plants of yesteryear, and again focused on the installation of panic and safety doors at my law office. The concept arguably made sense, if the doors were installed backwards. After all, most of my clients, having been unjustly sued, were, when entering my building, in a panic to see me. Or did it indeed make sense to install them properly to accommodate my clients' next move after they learned my fee?

I was about to ask these three men for a waiver of the section of the safety code that required installation of a metal panic door at my office. But these were the very men whose bureaucratic existence seemed predicated solely upon the compulsion that every door in Pennsylvania, even those serving one-seater outhouses, should have a panic bar attached.

They called for my case to be heard: "Labor and Industry vs. Fox." I stood up and walked to the seat of thousands of long-forgotten defendants and other condemned property owners.

"Mr. Fox ... " the head bureaucrat began.

"Yes ... "

"We have studied the photos of your office front door..."

"You have?"

"Yes. You are granted a waiver. You will not be required to install panic doors. You are excused."

That was it? I had driven 87 miles to hear one sentence? On the other hand, I had prevailed, so I gratefully thanked the three wise men, and dashed out of the room before they changed their minds.

I ran down four flights of stairs, rushed into the lobby, and flew out the door, which, thank goodness, was equipped with a panic bar.

CHAPTER NINE:
THE DERMATOLOGIST

This little *thing* had existed on my upper arm for as long as I could remember. It had never grown bigger nor changed color. In fact, I paid no attention to it at all until the day I was soaking in the health club Jacuzzi, and two winded tennis players joined me. They were complete strangers, but that didn't dissuade them from making comments about my state of health. Both started staring at my arm. Left then right. Up then down. Better to look there than elsewhere, I thought.

"I see you got a little *thing* hangin' there. On your biceps, I mean," the first guy said. His bald head glistened with sweat.

The second guy chimed in. "Yeah. Will you look at that. I had one of them growing on my ass, but at least I had the sense to have it sliced off."

"What? The growth or your rear?"

"Yeah, funny, pal. But seriously, you should have that taken off, so it don't grow and kill you," said the first guy. His friend nodded up and down in silent agreement.

All of the sudden I was mortified. How many other people had seen this *thing* and never told me? For a moment I imagined them all gathered for my viewing at Kornheisel's Funeral Home. Everyone I know is there staring at my pale dead face. I'm wearing my brown suit - the one that never fit right in the shoulders.

"It was on his upper arm. I swear it tripled in size in a week," Aunt Ethel recalled. "Then, it killed him."

My friend Dennis was despondent.

"I remember seeing it once at the swimming pool. As God as my witness, I meant to tell him to have it looked at, but I forgot. Now he's dead."

My mind left Kornheisel's organ music and the fake candelabras with the plastic wax drippings, and returned to the Jacuzzi. I was still alive. There was still time. I raced home and grabbed the phone book.

"Let's see ... dental supplies ... dentists ... here it is ... dermatologists." There were two names: Dr. Fiorello Lambingo and Dr. Wilbur Zachmeister.

Lambingo's office was all the way across town. Too far to drive during heavy traffic. Zachmeister was just six blocks down on the left.

"Doctor's office."

A real person. Thank goodness.

"Hi, my name is Larry Fox. I'd like to talk with the doctor about this *thing* that's - "

"What?! You dare to seek favor and speak with the Great and Powerful Oz? No one speaks with the Wizard. NO ONE!"

"But I've journeyed so far and if I can't talk to him, I may never get back home again to Auntie Emm."

My ruby red slippers weren't working at full speed. The receptionist was becoming impatient. "I said *How were you referred here*?"

"Uh. Yes. The yellow pages."

"I see ... In *that* case, the doctor's next available appointment is Tuesday, November 10th at 9:45 a.m. O.K.?"

"O.K.? How the hell is that O.K.? It's April 7th! I might be dead by then. What about my *thing*?"

She wanted nothing to do with my *thing*.

"Sir, I'm waiting."

This was no time to be indecisive. If I hesitated, the next appointment might not occur until after the President called with my nomination to the Supreme Court.

"I'll take it!" I stammered.

"Not so fast, mister. First I need to see if you qualify!"

"Qualify? Of course I qualify! I have a *thing*. It's growing on my - "

"Let's just run through a few questions first. Shall we? What kind of insurance do you have?"

Interesting question. I don't ever recall asking any potential client of mine if he or she had "legal insurance" to cover my bill. I always just hoped the accused bank robber du jour had enough money left over after the heist to pay me. The clients who were indicted for passing worthless checks ... now they were the ones who kept me up at night. I usually asked them for cash.

"Well, are you?"

"What?"

"Covered?"

"I have Blue Cross and Blue Shield through the County Bar Association. Does that help?"

"I'm almost positive they won't reimburse us for initial visits. I'll need the name of your bank, your social security number, business address, home phone, business phone, cell phone, fax number, name of closest friend or relative not living with you, a copy of your most recent credit card statement, permission to pull a credit report, confirmation that any bankruptcy proceedings have been concluded, your date of birth, and finally your racial grouping."

"Racial grouping?"

"This office deals with skin, Mr. Fox. The doctor needs to know skin color in advance. A gynecologist would want to know if you were a transsexual, no?"

I was in the wrong racket. I could just imagine pulling this stunt with my clients:

"Hello. Is the lawyer there?"

"Who's calling," my receptionist would ask, as she struggled to talk and apply nail polish at the same time.

"Felonious Indigent."

"Well, Mr. Indigent, he never talks to anybody directly. He's too busy cashing clients' certified checks at the bank. Is there something I can help you with?"

"I just got arrested for a felony. And I'm indigent. The preliminary hearing is next week, so I need to see him pronto!"

"Well, I'm looking over Attorney Fox's schedule and the best we can do is late next summer."

"But I may have been executed by then!"

"In that case, I do have here the number for Kornheisel's Funeral Home, if that helps."

I acquiesced, and gave the receptionist all of my information. She hung up. It was then I realized the one question she hadn't bothered to ask was why I needed a dermatologist in the first place.

So time went by. Every day for six months I looked at the *thing* on my arm, to see if it had grown during the night. It hadn't, and so I was still alive on Tuesday, November 10th. I showed up 15 minutes early. I didn't want to miss my designated time with the busy doctor. I opened the door and found some 30 other people already waiting. There wasn't a single seat. Not a single magazine. The air was thick with human breath. The receptionist in the glass observation booth refused to lift her head to see who I was. She opened a slit in the bulletproof partition, shoved a clipboard in my direction, and motioned for me to sit down. Then she returned to her phone call:

"Well, the next available appointment is in April. Do you have full health insurance? ... Oh, that's too bad ... Where do you bank?"

I wandered past a guy with a pimple the size of a walnut perched on the end of his nose. Poor soul. He had probably been waiting months to have it removed. I wasn't feeling so sorry for myself anymore. I inched into a corner, leaned against a wall, and began to study this rather personal questionnaire. And to think, I hadn't even met the doctor yet.

"How did your father die?"

"How did your mother die?"

"When did you last have a rash? Where?"

"Have you been here before? Why?"

And on the very bottom of the last page was a blank line long enough to fit a zip code. It said:

"Why are you here today? Please be brief."

That last question caught my attention, since I was beginning to think the good doctor didn't actually care about my potentially fatal *thing*.

About an hour rolled by, and they had begun to thin out the waiting room. While I read the latest article in a year old issue of "Dermatologist Monthly," the guy with the walnut nose was whisked into a secret chamber, and emerged 10 minutes later with a big bandage where the growth had been. He had to pay at the glass window, which was difficult for him, since he couldn't simultaneously write a check and hold what was left of his proboscis.

"Mr. Fox, Doctor will see you now," a snappy nurse advised me. I was both thrilled and apprehensive. Sure, I had graduated from the Waiting Room, but what would happen in the Examination Room? Maybe the *thing* was O.K. after all, just where it was. What if this physician yanked off my *thing* and I dropped dead? I thought about my poor family and my poor secretarial staff, left behind with all those incomplete files on the floor. I could just hear it:

"Hi.   Is the lawyer in?   I know I don't have an appointment, but this will just take a minute. I only have one little question."

"He died yesterday (sob). The dermatologist cut off his thing, and that was the end of him. Within two hours, he was dead."

"Oh my God! That's awful! Say, is there another lawyer here I could talk to?"

And then I wondered what would the examination room look like. Similar to a barber shop, would there be little warts and *things* piled up on the floor near the operating table?

I entered the inner sanctum from stage left. Zachmeister entered from stage right through a secret door utilized solely by him. Important people have private doors. Priests have access to the pulpit through an exclusive mysterious door; judges use the hidden door behind the bench. I have no such door.

The doctor looked the part with his white coat and trailing nursing assistant. But he was missing the shiny circular reflector head strap, so I was slightly disappointed. Still, for the blushing 34-year-old that he was, he commanded that unmistakable unspoken respect. His staff walked on eggshells around him. I had a staff, too, a staff I might never see again. My receptionist had always been so helpful ...

"Did anyone make coffee this morning? I don't think there's any milk either."

"Well, Larry, why don't you walk across the street to the minimart and see if they have any left?"

"That's not a bad idea. I'll be right back."

"Time to get naked, Mr. Fox. What'll it be today, pants or shirt?"

"I have this *thing* on my arm," I advised.

"Then by all means keep your pants on!"

The somber nurse giggled on cue, and hung my shirt on a hook as Doctor examined my arm.

"This is what we call a 'skin tag,' Mr. Fox. If you want, I can remove it.

"O.K."

He picked up some electrical device, made contact with my arm, and in less than two seconds, the *thing* had vanished in a little puff of smoke.

No wonder there were no warts on the floor.

"Any questions, feel free to call my staff," he said as he offered a quick handshake.

"Thanks, Doc," I said. "To be honest, I thought I was a dead man. I'm just happy everything's O.K."

"You were that worried?" he asked. "You should have come in sooner."

CHAPTER TEN:
THE PLEDGE

Maxwell Frank had for 55 years been a sole practitioner in the same office located across from the courthouse in Easton, Pennsylvania. The cemeteries are full of indispensable people, and with the exception of Queen Victoria, few individuals have remained effective after lingering at the same job more than half a century. Nonetheless, Maxwell tottered to work every blessed day, whereupon he would verbally dictate something or other to his loyal 82-year-old secretary. Maxwell had never quite figured out how to use newfangled electronic voice machines, but it didn't seem to matter. As he had grown older, he spoke slower, which was a good thing, since his secretary's shorthand wasn't quite as nimble as in days of yore.

There was no financial reason for Maxwell to work. He had been saving money since the Great Depression, just in case he needed some. Rumor had it that he was the millionaire next door, though you'd never know it from his clothes, car, or office furniture. He was a widower, and childless. With the exception of his secretary, there was no one in his life.

Maxwell was smoking one of his wretched hand-rolled cigars when the phone rang. Since both Maxwell and his office smelled like a cigar, his clientele was limited to those of a similar tobacco-tolerant persuasion. He picked up the heavy black 1947 receiver, ready to take the first call of the day. Perhaps the only call of the day. His secretary no longer answered the phone - not since the onset 10 years ago of arthritis in her right shoulder.

"Hello?"

"Maxwell? Is that you?"

"Yes. Who the hell is this?"

"Sidney. Sidney Stein."

"Counselor. How nice to hear from you. What case can I help you with?"

"No legal matter, Max. I'm calling on a personal request."

The two attorneys had known each other for 20 years. They worshiped at the same synagogue.

"Max, the rabbi asked me to call you since we missed you at temple last week."

"I had the flu, but I'm better now."

"I'm glad to hear that. Anyway, as you know, The United Jewish Appeal ends next week, and we're hopeful of achieving our goal. But we need one more significant pledge to go over the top. Max, we could use your help."

"Anything for you and the rabbi, Sid. You know that. How can I assist?"

"Max, we need a BIG favor ... "

"Name it."

"Will you pledge $5,000?" Sidney inquired tentatively.

"Consider it done," came Maxwell's unhesitating response.

"Max," Sidney gushed, "I can't thank you enough. The rabbi will be touched by your magnanimous gesture."

"Glad to help," Maxwell assured him.

"Can you bring the check to temple this Saturday? The campaign ends next week."

"You bet. Saturday," Maxwell echoed.

The next Monday, Maxwell's phone rang again - a rare occurrence. Maxwell answered the call, since his secretary's arthritis had not improved.

"Hello?"

"Maxwell? Is that you?"

"Yes. Who the hell is this?"

"Sidney. Sidney Stein. I missed you at temple on Saturday."

"I caught a cold, but I'm better now."

"I'm glad to hear that, Max. By the way, the rabbi wondered if you had sent in your check for $5,000. This year's United Jewish Appeal has ended."

"Tell the rabbi, the check is in the mail."

"Thanks, Max. Hope to see you at temple this Saturday."

The following Monday, Sidney called his friend, Maxwell once again. Max picked up the phone, because his secretary's arthritis wasn't any better.

"Hello?"

"Maxwell? Is that you?"

"Yes. Who the hell is this?"

"Sidney. Sidney Stein. Max, did you have a chance to send in your check? The rabbi asked me about it again. We didn't see you at services."

"I had the gout. I'll be there next week."

"Can I come by your office and pick up the check today?"

Maxwell became reflective for a moment. "Sid ... "

"Yes ... "

"When I made that $5,000 pledge, how did that make you feel?"

"Ecstatic."

"How about the rabbi? How did it make him feel?"

"Ecstatic, too!"

"Well, can't you consider that payment enough?"

CHAPTER ELEVEN:
THE VISITOR FROM A FAR OFF LAND

Scoundrels have been stealing from the dead since the beginning of time. Most notably, the treasures of the Egyptian pharaohs locked away in the pyramids, have been the objects of countless plunderers. Oscar Genevese was such a thief. After his uncle died, Oscar entered the decedent's home, and without authority, spirited away numerous valuables and cash he claimed had been promised to him. I represented the legitimate heirs of the estate, who sued for return of the assets.

I won't go to trial unless I believe my client will win. Why expend time, money, and effort if failure is the foreseeable result? My case was strong, my clients had been damaged, and the trial judge, President Judge Albert Williams, quickly sensed that Genevese was a wrongdoer who deserved to be surcharged. The two-day non-jury trial ended with an order directing that the stolen items be returned to the estate. My clients having been vindicated thanked me for my representation.

Although Judge Williams had served on the Northampton County Court for more than a decade, this was my first trial before him. As the President Judge, his administrative duties had often precluded him from engaging in protracted litigation. Only as a result of this hearing had I inadvertently gained the opportunity to study this jurist as he presided over the trial. He was intelligent, energetic, and focused. His reputation as a scholar of the law was well-deserved. And he looked the part. Aristocratic white hair, imposing posture and piercing eyes. He never let stewardship of the courtroom slip from his confident control.

Still, something was missing. He never smiled. Not once did he interject an off-handed comment to cut the tension of the proceedings. He worked by the book, completely devoid of humor and warmth.

I soon began to pack up my files in preparation for the journey back to the office. One of the tipstaffs approached me as I stood alone in the courtroom.

"The judge would like to see you in chambers."

I had tarried a moment too long. Although I was dog-tired from the stress of the litigation, this was not an invitation to be ignored. Was my hesitation that obvious?

"His Honor is waiting," the impatient tipstaff advised me.

Unlike His Honor, I have never possessed intimidating power over another human being, not even those on my payroll. Rather, at my law office, it's survival of the fittest. I remember once asking my receptionist to tell one of the secretaries to come to my office. She gave me one of those *who gives a shit - tell her yourself* looks, which I immediately obeyed.

I was led down the secret passageway that commenced behind the judge's bench, and ended at his chambers. The tipstaff rapped on the polished walnut door.

"Enter," a Thespian voice responded. I did as commanded.

There, in all his splendor, sat solemn all-powerful Judge Williams. An undeniable air of both juris and prudence permeated the atmosphere. A picture of His Honor having coffee with the President of the United States was hung just below His Honor's Harvard and Yale diplomas, along with the official seal of Northampton County. What did this omnipotent being want with me?

"Won't you sit down, Larry," the judge offered as he pointed to an authentic Chippendale chair. I inched toward the decorative furniture.

"You did a good job at trial," he noted. "Opposing

counsel for the defendant should have settled the case long ago."

That remark put me at ease and I sat down. Something warm, wet, and sticky immediately enveloped my ass cheeks. I shot out of the seat and looked downward in horror. The chair was drenched in vomit, and now so was I.

The judge sprang from his judicial recliner behind his antique desk, and dashed to my rescue. He appeared mortified, as I kept turning around like a dog chasing its tail, trying to ascertain the extent of the damage.

"I can't imagine how that mess - " he tried to explain. "I am *so* sorry."

I don't know who felt worse - the elusive individual who had become ill in chambers, the judge, or me. Funny though ... there was no stench, and as I felt my fanny, I couldn't actually feel much moisture. In fact, my pants were dry. The judge's lips began to quiver and his tipstaff began to smirk. Then they both burst out laughing.

"Gotcha good," His Honor observed between deep breaths. "Five and dime fake vomit, but it's worth a million laughs!"

Judge Williams reached down to retrieve the artificial blob of regurgitated goo that was cleverly connected to a hidden electrical cord.

"It's the newest model," he bragged. "You plug it in to keep it sticky and warm. Ain't it a killer?"

"A killer," I responded.

"Please do be seated," His Honor implored between subsiding guffaws.

I looked around for more traps. Seeing none, I gingerly sat in a different chair, as the judge returned to his desk. He wiped away a tear shed at my expense and then faced me.

"I heard that you perform amateur stand-up comedy on occasion. True?"

Oh no. The cat had leapt out of the bag. This was my hobby. A secret. A secret especially from my clients. The last thing they needed was to think that their attorney was a clown. That would be the same as learning my dentist was a professional mud wrestler. I'd never again feel the same about having her fingers in my mouth. So as a precautionary measure, I only performed 50 miles or more from home. But I couldn't lie to the judge. After all, we had bonded through vomit.

"Yes ... I perform stand-up comedy ... on occasion," I hesitated.

"Outstanding," His Honor interjected. "I'll get right to the point. The court needs a favor."

I gulped. I had just finished a tough trial. I played the fake vomit game. Now I was about to get whacked again.

"I'd be delighted," I heard myself assure the judge.

A wide grin spread across his face. What had I agreed to do? He turned to his tipstaff.

"Excuse us for a moment."

The servant of the court nodded, and disappeared. What sinister plot was about to unfold?

"Do you know any professional comedians?" Judge Williams inquired.

"Yes, I've met quite a few in my travels."

"Excellent. Now here's what's on my mind. In about four months, our bar association will celebrate its 150th anniversary. As you know, we are one of the oldest bar associations in the country, and the occasion will be marked by a formal black-tie dinner sponsored by the Bench and attended by the Bar. I expect that more than 200 attorneys and judges will take part in the festivities at the country club. You're planning to be there?"

"Yes," I confirmed.

"Perfect. Now an event of this magnitude requires a guest speaker of international proportion, wouldn't you agree?"

He was the judge and I was imprisoned in his chambers. There was but one answer.

"Of course, Your Honor."

"Good. I was thinking of inviting the Chief Justice of

the International World Court at The Hague to address our gathering."

That would be impressive. Apparently not only did Judge Williams take coffee with presidents - he was also connected to members of the International Court.

"Of course," he continued, "I don't know the Chief Justice of the World Court from a hole in the wall, and even if we sent him a free plane ticket, the pompous ass would no doubt decline," Judge Williams lamented. "That's where you come in."

"Me? Your Honor, I don't even know the night janitor at the municipal building."

"No. I suppose you wouldn't. Regardless. You need to find a comedian to impersonate The Hague's Chief Justice."

"I beg your pardon?"

"And I don't want him to be too funny at first. Everyone at the dinner - at least for the first 15 minutes or so - should believe the speaker is genuine. Then he'll drop a few hints that he's an impostor. We'll see if anyone catches on. It'll be a hoot, just like the vomit."

Judge Williams' animated eyes sparkled as he waited for my response. I had to admit the idea was intriguing. It might well be an evening to remember. The judge sensed he had snared his catch and so he reeled in the line.

"There's $1,000 in the budget. Can you find the right guy?"

The right guy? There were starving comedians who would have taken the job for 50 bucks. Some would have paid $100 just for the chance to appear on stage. Any stage. I was in.

"Of course, you must never speak of this," Judge Williams cautioned. "And depending how things unfold that evening, I may blame you for everything. However it ends, though, remember you'll always have my silent and unending gratitude."

We shook hands to bind the clandestine plot. The judge returned the fake vomit to his desk drawer, ready for its next victim.

Finding the right comedian was a snap. I called Ezekiel, the same theatrical agent who scheduled my comedy club appearances. I told him what I needed, similar to ordering up a blind date from one of those matchmaker services.

"No problem, pal. You want this here Chief Justice to have an accent?"

"Dutch."

"Pennsylvania Dutch?"

"No. Holland Dutch."

"How old?"

"About 45."

"Bald?"

"It doesn't matter. But he should look wealthy."

"Any special costume, or will a business suit suffice?"

"It's a black-tie affair. He has to wear a tuxedo."

Indeed, this dinner would be more formal than the academy awards. And when word spread that the guest speaker was none other than "The Honorable Henrique X. Von Carrien, Supreme Justice of the International Court at The Hague, Netherlands," there was a run at the local formal wear rental shop. R.S.V.P.s began to flood the bar association office. The country club would have to remove the retractable walls separating the two largest dining rooms.

I had retained comedian Al Nolt for the evening's festivities. The booking agent gave me Nolt's telephone number, and told me to negotiate any specific contractual terms directly with him. There was no time to lose. I called Nolt that very evening.

"This is Larry Fox. Is Mr. Nolt available?"

"He's just finishing up with another client. May I take down some preliminary information."

I was impressed. His staff was polite and his services

were in demand. Soon Al picked up.

"Al Nolt. How can I help you?"

I explained about the chief justice of the international world court. Was he available that night? Could he pull off the accent? Could he mingle with judges?

"You bet," Al answered. "By the way, am I paying to perform, or are you paying me?"

"We're paying you. And we'll rent your tuxedo, if you don't have one."

"Great. How long do I talk?"

"Half an hour. You'll discuss life as the chief justice. I want you to be funny, but not at first. We need to convince everyone that you are the real deal. I'll mail you a profile on him, and maybe you can look up some information on the web."

"Sounds good. This will be a piece of cake. I had an uncle once who attended law school for almost a year, so if they ask me any questions, I'll be prepared."

I gave Al directions to the country club from his home in Freehold, New Jersey.

"I'll see you in a couple of weeks," he confirmed. "You'll be able to pick me out. I'll be the guy with the gray hair, glasses, and the accent."

- - - - - - - - - - - - - - - - - - - -

This would, indeed, be an evening to remember. The sesquicentennial of the bar association was an historic milestone, and the presence of the Chief Justice of the International World Court gave the occasion even greater significance. Everyone was there. Three federal judges, two state superior court jurists, eight common pleas members of the court, and nearly 200 attorneys.

I found myself in a sea of mingling tuxedos. Since I had been instrumental in securing the presence of the guest speaker, Judge Williams reserved a place for me at one of the circular dignitaries' tables near the speaker's podium. I had never dined with such lofty personages.

The six plush red velvet seats were occupied by Judge Williams, Federal Judge Hershey, Commonwealth Court Judge Sylvester, Anthony Risuto, the President of the Northampton County Bar Association, and me. An open chair remained poised for the arrival of Al Nolt. I sat fidgeting with what I hoped was my salad fork, as these pillars of the judicial community discussed legal issues amongst themselves.

The pecking order was clearly observed without the need for a word of clarification. When the federal judge opened his mouth, even to take a bite of something, everyone else froze. Next in line was Commonwealth Court Judge Sylvester, then Judge Williams, and finally the Bar Association President. As a person or lawyer, I didn't count, so I kept quiet. If and when Nolt, a/k/a Von Carrien arrived, protocol demanded that he, of course, ascend to the top of the pecking order.

I continued to fidget. Where the hell was Nolt? Probably still stuck on Route 22. The other dignitaries didn't seem to notice.

"The new federal courthouse should be built within the next two years," Judge Hershey proclaimed. "The President's final budget goes to Congress next month." The other judges nodded in agreement.

A waitress approached me, probably because I was using the wrong soup spoon.

"A Mr. Von Carrien is here to see you," she whispered. "He's in the foyer."

There was a God. I waited until all the judges' mouths shut simultaneously, and then excused myself. I trotted out to the hallway, to find the comedian whom I had not previously met. There stood Al Nolt, part-time comic, and tonight, full-time Chief Justice of the World Court. He was pulling at the rented suspenders holding up his rented pants. For somebody who had never even adjudicated the merits of a parking ticket violation, he definitely looked the part. He was about 55, had some gray hair, and wore bifocals. I stuck out my hand.

"Thanks for coming."

"Glad to be here. In New Jersey, we have exit numbers. You should tell them to put exit numbers on the highway ramps here." Perhaps Al might, during dinner conversation, suggest to Federal Judge Hershey that he ask the President to place that request in the congressional budget.

"C'mon. I'll introduce you to the folks at your table," I proposed. Our two rented tuxedos approached four judges and a bar association president.

"It is with pleasure that I present to the Court and its guests the Honorable Henrique X. Von Carrien, Chief Justice of the International Court at The Hague, Netherlands," I announced. If one of these guys had asked to see some ID, we would have been cooked. Al's New Jersey driver's license wouldn't have gotten us far. Everyone stood up. Judge Williams, my co-conspirator, winked at me. Federal Judge Hershey had first peck.

"It is indeed a pleasure to meet you, Your Honor," he acknowledged.

"The pleasure is all mine," Nolt responded in a genteel British accent he only now began to utilize.

"I would have expected a Dutch accent," Judge Hershey observed.

"I was raised in the British West Indies," the Chief Justice explained.

"How fascinating," Judge Sylvester interjected as introductions were concluded and everyone took his seat.

"How long will you be visiting our country?" Hershey inquired, as a waitress appeared with the main course, filet mignon and lobster.

"Oh my!" the Chief Justice exclaimed in his impeccable British tongue. "You folks sure know how to eat! Back home, it's usually cold cuts - maybe some coleslaw for good measure. But I digress. I've been asked to present lectures at a few universities, and at the United Nations. Then I will return to the Hague for the next term of court."

"What are the topics of your lectures?" Attorney Risuto questioned.

"International law and the comparison between various concepts of jurisprudence presently utilized in the civilized world."

Judge Williams and I looked at each other in silent surprise, for it appeared our impostor might be able to go toe-to-toe with these heavyweights.

"What particular insight will you seek to impart to those attending your lectures?" Judge Sylvester queried.

"That's an interesting question," the Chief Justice responded as he closely inspected a cut of steak impaled on the end of his fork. "If I've learned anything from my years on the bench, it's that international law is in a constant state of flux, and yet the foundations of the law within each state remain constant. As an example, in Russia, everything is prohibited - even that which should be permitted. In the United States, everything is permitted except that which is prohibited. In France, everything is permitted, including that which should be prohibited. Once such patterns become evident, the study of international law is relatively simple."

"Fascinating!" Judge Sylvester exclaimed again, as the Chief Justice munched on his filet.

"My compliments to the chef," Al offered.

"How long has the court existed?" Federal Judge Hershey inquired.

"We received our initial charter from the United Nations in 1953. At that time we were known as the 'World Court.' Later on we became 'The International Court' and why not? If the *House of Pancakes* can go international, why not us?" The Chief Justice laughed out loud and began to attack the lobster.

"Fascinating," Judge Sylvester repeated. "Tell me, Judge, what gives rise to most of the cases you hear?"

"Money troubles - that's what. Countries squabbling with each other over who owes what to whom. The simple days of the two Ukrainian villages doing each other's laundry to make a couple extra bucks are long gone. Now everything is an international monetary crisis."

"Are you permitted to discuss any pending case involving such an issue?" Judge Hershey asked.

"Oh, sure," Nolt assured the federal judge with a wave of his hand. Then he took another bite of lobster as he simultaneously fielded the question. "Presently, we're hearing a complex matter involving the positive retention of negative cash flow. Uganda says the funds belong to it. Mozambique takes the opposite view."

"Fascinating," Judge Sylvester chimed in yet again.

"How can a country retain money that doesn't exist?" Hershey, always the pragmatist, interjected. It was clear why he had risen to the status of a federal judgeship.

"It happens all the time," Nolt assured him. "As you are aware, Bethlehem Steel recently filed for protection in Federal Bankruptcy Court, but that didn't stop its executives from petitioning for bonuses, which the court granted."

Judge Hershey began to squirm in his seat as Nolt pursued and claimed another cut of steak. It disappeared into his mouth.

"I'll give you guys another example: sometimes one nation agrees to lend money to another. The question often arises regarding interest due on funds that may not presently exist."

"What exactly does that mean?" Attorney Risuto inquired with a perplexed look on his face.

"Simple," Nolt began. "Suppose three brothers stop at a hotel for the night. They share one room for $30. Each brother gives the clerk $10. The brothers retire for the night. But then the honest clerk realizes he mistakenly charged too much - it's only a $25 room. The clerk gives the bellhop five $1 bills and tells the bellhop to deliver the five bills to the three brothers. The dishonest bellhop decides to keep $2 as his tip. He gives each brother $1. As a result, each brother has only paid $9 for the room." Nolt began a pointed search in the covered bread basket for another muffin.

"So what!" Judge Hershey exclaimed.

"Well," Nolt continued, "nine times three equals 27.

The bellhop kept $2. That's $29. Where's the other dollar? The answer, of course, is that this represents the positive retention of negative cash flow."

Hershey and Sylvester looked at each other as President Judge Williams began to rise from his seat to make the evening's introductions.

"I think it's time I begin tonight's program," he suggested, as he made his way to the podium positioned at the front of the huge room. There was enthusiastic applause.

"Honorable judges, legal counsel, and guests, it will be my great pleasure in a few moments to introduce tonight's guest speaker, Henrique X. Von Carrien, Judge of the International World Court at The Hague. But first, as is our annual custom, the time has arrived to honor those of our membership who have reached their 50th year as members of the Northampton County Bar. Tonight, we honor Bertrum Hunsberger. Making the presentation will be bar association President Anthony Risuto."

Risuto approached the podium and turned to gaze upon the sea of faces. He knew everyone in the room by name.

"Ladies and gentlemen, I just visited 'ol' Berty' at the nursing home on Tuesday, and if he had been able to speak, I'm sure he would have remarked how much he enjoyed receiving the engraved silver plated anniversary bowl."

There was polite applause for a lawyer few could remember.

"He'll probably use it as a bed pan," an attorney seated near me at the next table mumbled to a friend as Judge Williams continued.

"Ladies and gentlemen, and judges of our several courts, it gives me great pleasure to introduce tonight's guest speaker, Henrique X. Von Carrien, Chief Justice of the International Court at The Hague, Netherlands. The Chief Justice is not only a recognized scholar of international law, but also the author of several acclaimed books and treatises, including *The System Paradigm of Introspection, The Metaphysics of Denial and Pathos,*

Jurisprudence Among the Primates, and the New York Times best seller *A History of the Moral Epicenter Revisited.* Won't you join me in giving our guest a warm Northampton County welcome."

And everyone did, so Nolt grabbed one final bite of steak, and strode to the microphone as he chewed.

"Thank you so much for inviting me," he began. "At the outset, let me begin by defining the jurisdictional scheduling parameters of the World Court. Disputes arising below the equator are heard by us prior to when the earth reaches the apex of the northern summer solstice. Disputes arising above the equator are scheduled after the earth has passed beyond the vinculum of the southern winter solstice. In this way, confusion is avoided."

"Fascinating," Judge Sylvester was heard to say.

"Of course, as President Judge of the World Court, I have several administrative duties, in addition to the usual judicial functions. As an example, I monitor legal fees charged. Not every country that appears as a litigant before the World Court can afford to pay counsel. Those with operating budgets in the red, for instance, sometimes qualify for public defenders. If we can sidebar for a second, here, personally, I view legal fees as similar to sex. Most lawyers think they simply aren't getting enough, and that everyone else is getting more than they deserve. I try to even things out whenever possible."

"I never thought about it exactly that way before," Judge Sylvester pondered out loud.

"I also monitor dress code in my courtroom. You know, when Napoleon rode into battle, he always wore a red uniform so that even if he were wounded, no one could tell. And that's the reason today I think so many lawyers wear brown pants. Know what I mean?"

"And just today, I toured your local courthouse. It must be tough practicing law around here. They had reserved spaces in the parking deck for any old schmuck, from the animal control officer to the assistant night janitor. Funny though, I didn't see any area set aside for you poor slobs. But that sorta makes sense. When I got to the front door of the courthouse, the sign said *No Solicitors.* "

I looked at Judge Williams. He looked at me.

"By the way," Nolt continued, "before I forget, here's my favorite lawyer joke. Stop me if you've heard this one:

> *This guy is walking on the beach, and he finds a magic lantern, so he rubs it and a genie appears.*
>
> *"You get three wishes, master," the genie says, "but take note - whatever you wish for will be granted, but every lawyer in the world will receive twice as much."*
>
> *"That's O.K. with me," the guy agrees. "First, I want a million dollars."*
>
> *"Granted, but every lawyer in the world now has two million."*
>
> *"Next, I want a Rolls Royce limo."*
>
> *"Granted, but every lawyer in the world now owns two of them."*
>
> *"Finally, I'd like to donate one of my kidneys to medical science."*

One of the younger lawyers seated at the table behind me wasn't quite as impressed with Nolt as was Judge Sylvester.

"Hey," he yelled out. "I think this guy's trying to insult us!"

"What gives you that impression?" Nolt responded. "Just because you practice law in stinko Bethlehem? Today I was watching the Weather Channel. They got the weather for Scranton, Wilkes-Barre, and Fort Indiantown Gap. No Bethlehem. Does that give you an idea why Billy Joel named the song *Allentown* instead?"

"Who does this guy think he is?" another angry lawyer called out. Obviously, this attorney didn't plan to appear in the near future before the World Court.

Judge Sylvester was beginning to look confused. Judge Williams, possessor of the fake vomit and instigator of tonight's farce, looked squarely at me and I at him. Nolt was still on a roll. When was someone going to figure out that the emperor had no clothes?

"Not only do we hear international litigation arising between sovereign nations, but it appears our review has already begun to reach into the interplanetary realm. The United States has refused to pay mounting storage fees for the lunar buggy it continues to park on the moon. Well, there ain't no free lunch, now is there? Everyone in this room knows what happens if you ignore a parking ticket."

The polite audience was turning into a restless crowd.

"Maybe we better get outa here," Williams whispered to me.

"But Nolt ... he may be in danger," I pleaded.

"He's a big boy. He got in this mess. He can get out."

We both left by the side door. Nolt was just beginning to give his reasoning as to why Bethlehem Steel went bankrupt.

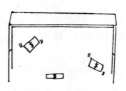

CHAPTER TWELVE:
THE VIEW FROM UNDER THE TABLE

Clancy's Diner was located on a back road between Howertown and Jacksonville, Pennsylvania. It had been there since time began, and had a steady clientele for years. After the construction of a super highway by-pass, the only remaining customers were the regulars who knew the pies were baked on the premises, and the prices were 20 years behind the times. And it was as if time stood still inside. Original miniature table-top juke boxes at each booth still offered three songs for a quarter. Pink plastic curtains still decorated the windows. And the menu offerings were the same as a generation or two ago. Outside, the polished stainless steel exterior and green tinted windows always gleamed, even in the evening hours. A few times the diner almost closed its doors for good. But luckily for the loyal coffee and pie crowd, that never happened.

The place was an optical illusion. From the outside it looked relatively small. Inside it was expansive. Seasoned customers read the day's news as they perched themselves on an endless row of swivel stools that stretched from one end of the diner all the way to the other. Mike, the chef, manned the grill in full view of the clientele who often spoke up when they wanted their eggs flipped.

The customers and waitresses knew each other by name, even though the three ladies who labored as servers never wore name tags. Their neatly pressed blue and white uniforms bore the single name "Clancy's," embroidered in cursive style on the upper left pocket. Any customer, whether a regular or a stranger, male or female, was addressed the same way: "Honey." And since this diner was located in Eastern Pennsylvania, any question posed always ended with the word "then."

"Honey, will that be all *then*?"

"Sam, Honey, you want more coffee *then*?"

Rumor has it that once upon a time, there actually was a "Clancy." But that was four million eggs ago. Now Mike was running the show - 12 hours a day, seven days a week. He did, however, close on Christmas and Easter, in an attempt to enjoy at least one or two home-cooked meals during the year.

Thelma had worked there for the last seven years. She was the one who wore too much lipstick. It was anyone's guess how old she was, since she was in great physical shape. After all, she walked at a spirited pace at least five miles a day within the confines of the diner that time had forgotten - something equivalent to running the 100 yard dash inside a telephone booth. She wore out at least one pair of sneakers each month, even though she had never stepped foot on a tennis court nor taken leisurely walks through her neighborhood. She was too busy trying to make a living. Despite all this running around, her styled blond wig held tight to her head and never budged. Maybe she had gray hair, maybe no hair, but the wig enabled her to maintain an ageless 30-something mystique. During a rare quiet moment, she and the other two servers, Rosie and Peggy, would sit on the three stools near the deep fryer and chat quietly while filling the shakers until their next customer walked in.

Mike was lucky, and he knew it. His employees were honest. He could come and go throughout the day without issue. The cash stayed in the register and the steaks didn't walk from the freezer. The ladies shared a common work ethic, and believed in the seventh commandment. When Rosie once found a $5 bill on the floor under the last stool, she returned it the very next week when Mr. Scogin came in once again to take advantage of the all-you-can-eat pasta special.

One evening, just before closing time, Thelma took the garbage out while Rosie mopped a spill near the door. As fate would have it, on her way back in, Thelma slipped and fell to the floor, breaking her elbow. Next came emergency surgery, and three months of recuperation. She filed for worker's compensation.

Once in a while, I stopped at Clancy's for the apple crumb pie. It was made daily from both fresh apples and fresh crumbs. Mike, the owner, knew I was a lawyer, so when tragedy struck, he called.

"Hi. This is Mike."

"Forgive me. Do I know you?"

"From over at Clancy's Diner. I make the pies."

"Oh ... that Mike! It's so nice to hear from you, Mike. How's the diner business?"

"Not bad. People got to eat. Listen, I have a question..."

"Shoot."

"One of my waitresses, Thelma, fell at work last week and broke her elbow ... "

"That's a shame! By the way, is she the one who uses- "

"Yeah. Too much lipstick. Well anyway, now she needs a whole 90 days to recover, so she just filed for worker's compensation."

"That sounds logical. What's the problem?"

"Well, you see, actually she ain't really an employee. She's more like what you'd call one of them 'independent contractors.' That's the reason I've never had to carry no expensive worker's compensation insurance. It's a way to save money, so I can keep my prices low."

"Mike, how many hours a week does she work at the diner?"

"Maybe 50 or so, but they're all legitimate 'under the table' hours. See, she gets paid in cash, so she don't have to report nothing. That way, she saves money, too. I can't get nobody to waitress at the diner if I deduct taxes before I hand them a paycheck. Not to mention I'd have to pay 'em more, too."

During the next 10 minutes, I learned that his three full-time waitresses, all of whom worked overtime, did not exist anywhere on his books as employees. No taxes, no social security payments, no workers' compensation, and of course, no time-consuming deductions. Rather, these cumbersome computations were simply ignored.

"It's possible you may have a problem, Mike," I advised.

"That's the thing about you lawyers - always throwing a fly in the ointment. Don't you understand? If income is reported, it'll screw with the child support from Thelma's first husband. He pays, assuming she has no income."

"But if she earns money, her earnings statements are required to be submitted to the Domestic Relations Office."

"See?" Mike protested. "That's just what I mean. You're tipping the apple cart."

"Mike, there are more than just apples in your cart here."

"What's that supposed to mean?"

"It means, Mike, that it's a criminal offense for an employer to fail to carry worker's compensation insurance. You are personally liable for Thelma's medical expenses and a percentage of her lost earnings."

"Oh crap. That's just what I need. How much?"

A good question, indeed. If Thelma reported no income, her testimony at the time of the worker's compensation hearing would be crucial.

Mike decided to retain me, despite the fact that I was complicating things. Since he didn't have much money, it was agreed that I, as an independent contractor, would receive a fresh calorie-packed pie each week for an entire year as payment.

- - - - - - - - - - - - - - - - - - - -

"All rise," the tipstaff announced, as Henry Primrose, worker's compensation referee, entered the courtroom. Primrose presided over cases involving employees injured on the job, and the compensation to which they might be entitled. During his 15-year tenure as a referee, he had heard testimony about hundreds of tables under which thousands of non-employees had labored in secret.

The referee took a dim view of employers who willfully failed to pay the required worker's compensation contribution, a fact I made clear to my client. Mike and I were not there to dispute his statutory duty. Rather, the court needed to determine a dollar amount due Thelma. The only way to do that was to ascertain her actual net income - no easy task, since Thelma had engaged in her own rather convoluted accounting alchemy. She was called to the witness stand to help enlighten the court. She proceeded to the chair located next to the judge, her arm in a sling, her feet in worn out Keds. She raised her remaining usable arm.

"Do you intend to tell the Truth, and nothing but the Truth, so help you God?" the tipstaff asked.

"You betcha," she confirmed from her crimson-coated lips.

She was unrepresented by legal counsel, so His Honor initiated the direct examination.

"Ms. Pitchel, on the day of your injury, were you an employee of Clancy's Diner?"

"Sure was, Honey."

"How do you spell 'Pitchel'?" I asked my client in a whisper.

"I've never even heard her last name," Mike responded with a shrug of his shoulders. "Everybody just calls her Thelma."

"How long have you been so employed?" the court continued.

"Seven years, then."

"Are you a U.S. citizen, born in this country?"

"Me? Why, yes."

"How old are you?"

Up to this point in time, Thelma had been fielding inquiries with relative ease. Here's where she put on the brakes. She leaned toward the referee and mumbled something in his ear.

"O.K. Fair enough, Ms. Pitchel. That will be our little secret. Were you injured while at work?"

"Whizz, bang! Right on my elbow. Wanna sign the cast?" Thelma asked, relieved she had dodged the age question.

"How many hours do you work each week?"

"About 50. It depends then."

"On what?"

"The specials. Like liver and onions for $2.95. We get a crowd. I pick up some more hours."

"Are you paid by the hour?"

"Absolutely. Plus tips."

"What are you paid?"

"That's a hard one. See, Judge, I keep two sets of books. One is for the IRS and the Domestic Relations Office. I can't afford to pay taxes, so I work under the table. It really works out better for me if I under-report my income. The other set of books has the real figures, including tips. That's how I stick to my monthly budget."

This was the first time in my experience as an attorney that I had actually been present as a witness confessed under oath that she had committed multiple felonies: defrauding the federal, state, and local governments. But it was the irony of it all that struck me. My client had paid me so that I could pay my taxes, a portion of which went to pay for this referee to sit in judgment over my client and this witness, both of whom had failed to pay their proper share of taxes.

"Ms. Pitchel," the polite referee persisted, "how much do you earn?"

"Do you really need to know that? It's kind of personal."

"We *really* do. Actually, it's the reason we all stopped by here today - just so you might tell us."

"I don't know ... Like my age, I'm a little sensitive about giving out that kind of information, Judge. Can I whisper it?"

"I'm afraid not. Mr. Fox may want to know as well."

"What does he care? I'm the only one who's responsible for the taxes."

The judge was beginning to grow impatient. He motioned to me. "Mr. Fox, perhaps you might wish to cross-examine the petitioner."

I stood and approached the witness.

"Ms. Pitchel ..."

"What?"

"I represent Mike, the cook."

"Yeah, I know who you are, Honey. Pork and sauerkraut on Tuesdays. Good tipper. What can I do for you, then?"

"Ma'am, how much did you earn in tips last year?"

Her body language immediately turned defensive.

"Larry, you stand there with that judgmental lawyer face of yours, dressed in your $200 suit, using your $200 words. The only difference between you and me is you got to graduate from high school, and you had enough money to go to college and law school. I had to help keep a roof over the heads of my three brothers. Now I have two kids to raise by myself. If I don't pay all my so-called taxes, that's because I can't. The government would have just wasted the money on another space shuttle launch anyway. I need every dime I make to feed my kids. Besides, everyone does it. Is it really theft to shave a couple of pennies off your taxes? Are you going to stand there and tell me you don't do it, too?"

As a matter of fact, I had just sent a quarterly tax payment to the IRS. As a result, I didn't know how I would pay this week's office overhead, a chronic problem for the last 30 years. My used car needed a new muffler, the toilet at the office was leaking again, and someday I hoped to buy a new suit from the Men's Discount Warehouse because this one was 8 years old.

"Ms. Pitchel," I inquired, "how much money did you make during the last 12 months?"

Ultimately, the referee awarded Thelma compensation based on a figure higher than that reported to the IRS, but lower than the income tabulated in her secret second set of books. She decided not to appeal this decision, since she preferred that as little attention as possible be drawn to her unorthodox method of computing income.

As for Mike - at my urging, he retained an accountant, and initiated a new system of record keeping. The three waitresses were soon reflected as full-time employees. Deductions were taken for social security, income tax, and worker's compensation.

As a result, liver and onions, even when "on special," now cost $7.50, and a slice of homemade pie rose from $.50 a wedge to $1.75. And I did receive a pie for 52 straight weeks, payment now valued at $728. I reported this figure to the IRS, but I'm still debating deduction of $600 as a business expense - the cost of which covers two health club memberships that my secretary and I needed to offset our latest weight gain of 10 pounds each.

CHAPTER THIRTEEN:
THE INQUISITIVE COWS

The widow, Erma Gerhard, passed away recently. She and her husband, Clyde, had, for more than half of a century, maintained one of the sprawling dairy farms near Kriedersville, Pennsylvania. They had not been blessed with children, just cows. Like any parent, though, they knew well the individual quirks of each member of their herd. They lovingly provided them all with patient guidance.

This was remarkable for three reasons: there were more than 200 cows, each with its own name; the Gerhards issued various commands solely in Pennsylvania Dutch; and the cows responded obediently without fail. Obviously, the Gerhards learned long ago what many other farmers had not: cows only speak Pennsylvania Dutch. Those who never came to this realization were plagued with untrained, confused and incorrigible cows.

"Komm hier, Edvinna," Erma would coax, and lumbering Edvinna with the speckled udder, rather than Frederika with the dainty hooves, or Matilda with the longish tail, would advance into the milking stall. Once in a while, an impatient animal would try to squeeze in line.

"Nien, Hildegard!" Clyde would admonish. "Warten Zie dort." Hildegard would then stop and look about apologetically.

And so it was after many visits to the farm over the years, I learned that cows were highly intelligent, gentle animals. I enjoyed my sojourns to this tranquil place, and the Gerhards were always gracious hosts, even when my visits were for the purpose of reviewing some uncharted legal issue. A new contract for feed, grain, and hay, for instance, or the proposed lease of a harvesting machine often required my attention.

There was always a crock of homemade soup waiting for me in the expansive farmhouse kitchen.

"You are the only lawyer I know who makes house calls," Erma once observed.

I would have driven 100 miles for some of her chicken noodle soup. Her passing and the death of Clyde before her, meant more than the loss of a client or two. They had become good friends. I was now charged with the stewardship of their estate, which included the care, feeding, and daily milking of 200 cows, none of whom spoke a word of English.

Thankfully, the neighboring dairy farmer, Russell Moyer, graciously agreed to shoulder the temporary duties. No one was better suited for the job. He and his wife, Alice, resided just a quarter mile from the Gerhard farmhouse, which they could see from their dining room window. And they spoke Pennsylvania Dutch. I'd rest a lot easier knowing the cows would be cared for by someone with whom they could converse.

Two weeks after the funeral, I received an unexpected call from Russell. It was 9 o'clock on a Saturday night.

"Lawyer Larry?"

"Yes."

"This is Farmer Russell. I think you better get over to the Gerhard farm." His request sounded ominous.

"Is there something wrong?" I gasped.

"I'm not sure, but 60 or 70 of the cows I let out to graze for the night are staring into the Gerhard's kitchen window. Something's up. I'm going over to have a look."

I thanked Russell for his call, and jumped into my Buick. I arrived at the farm about 25 minutes later. The state police were already on scene, and had placed some ne'er-do-well in handcuffs in the back of their cruiser.

Russell made his curt introductions.

"Lawyer Larry. State Trooper VonStupen." We shook hands.

"Are you the attorney for the Gerhard estate?" the trooper asked.

"Yes," I affirmed. "Is there a problem?"

"Not anymore," the trooper related. "We just removed a burglar from the house. He was loading valuables into a truck he had parked around back.

Russell then began to relay the story. He and Alice had just settled in to watch reruns of *Dragnet* when they sensed something was wrong at the Gerhards. In the still of the summer night, they could see that the cows had pushed over a fence - something they would *never* do - and had moved as a large group toward the Gerhard's kitchen window. It was their location on the property, so near the homestead, that tipped off Russell.

"I went over to ask the cows what had caught their attention. 'Was geht's?' They all motioned toward the kitchen. That's when I saw the burglar, so I called the cops on my cell phone."

The cows had saved the farm. "Danke" I said to each one. The cows nodded their heads up and down in recognition of my appreciation.

CHAPTER FOURTEEN:
THE RECORD STORE

My secretary, Cathy, has always scheduled my appointments. A potential client will call. If the issue falls within my area of expertise, Cathy arranges the meeting. That makes my job simple. Similar to the client, all I need do is show up and listen.

It was Thursday morning. I opened the office promptly at 8:00 and quickly scanned my calendar. The day before, I had been at a protracted hearing that continued into the evening, and had yet to see the day's appointments. Cathy walked in two minutes later.

"Cathy?"

"Yes ... "

"I see you made three appointments for me today."

"Yes. The 10 o'clock is a simple will. Mrs. Gross is a widow with grown kids. She knew your mother and father."

"What about the 1 o'clock?"

"That's Horace Hinkel. You represented him when he bought his house on Laurel Street. Now he's selling and moving into a condo."

"And the 4 o'clock?"

"That's Conrad Schultz. He said he's an M.D. from Akron, Ohio. There was a death in his family, so it's an estate matter."

"Did I know the decedent?"

"I don't think so. It was a brother who lived here in town. A Melvin Schultz. I looked up the obituary. The funeral was two days ago. It appears that the doctor is the only surviving relative."

"How did he get my name?"

"Somebody at the viewing said he knew you."

Funny. I was born in this town, and with luck, I'll die here. I didn't know it at the time, but when I started kindergarten at age five, I had begun to forge relationships with future clients. The yellow pages are jammed with countless full-page ads for lawyers. Thank God I never had to waste good money on such nonsense.

The minute I laid eyes on Mrs. Gross, it all came back to me. She used to work as a clerk at city hall when I was an assistant city solicitor. It took 15 minutes to dictate her last will and testament. Then we sat and reminisced for over an hour about the good old days, before the new municipal complex was built.

At 1:00, Horace Hinkel stopped in. He had had a heart attack last year, and felt it was time to move into maintenance-free housing. I drafted a proposed agreement of sale. Horace was pleased that a young couple with a new baby was going to buy the place. "They'll be happy there," he sighed.

I unpacked the sandwich I had made for lunch, read two day's worth of mail, returned 10 calls, and remembered once again that my parents had been kind enough to bless me with a good education, and that I lived in a free country. Four o'clock rolled around quickly.

"Dr. Schultz is here," Cathy announced. "Shall I direct him into the conference room?"

"Yes." It was time to chronicle the passing of a fellow human being. Every estate contains the story of someone's unique life. In a small way, the decedent comes alive again in these meetings, through the words of surviving family members. What void had been created by the death of the doctor's brother? I grabbed a notepad, and made my way toward the conference room.

"Dr. Schultz?" I inquired. The doctor extended a manicured hand that had probably never shoveled snow, nor raked a lawn.

What type of medical doctor might he be? His eyes were closer together than normal, and he squinted a little, as if he often peered into the dark. There was only one obvious answer: proctologist.

"Pardon me for being so bold," he offered, "but I noted that the heel of your left shoe is worn down. Are you experiencing difficulty walking?"

"No," I assured my guest. "My dog just ate part of my shoe yesterday. It's his little way of telling me I was a half hour late."

"Forgive me for asking. You see, I'm a podiatrist."

"It's nice to make your acquaintance. What brings you to Bethlehem?"

"My brother Melvin's funeral. He just passed away." The doctor appeared genuinely upset.

"I'm sorry for your loss."

"Thank you. He was a good brother, even if he was a little strange."

Strange? I love strange. I re-adjusted myself and got comfortable.

"Doctor, when did your brother pass away?"

"Last Thursday. The funeral was this weekend."

I began to take notes. "Did he leave a last will and testament?"

Always an interesting question. What if there were only a "testament," but no "will"? Is that like assault without battery?

Dr. Schultz reached into his black doctor's bag on the floor. He produced a document protected by a faded parchment envelope, and handed it to me.

"This is it. My brother's will," he proclaimed.

I studied the 10-year-old instrument. "It appears that you, sir, are the sole beneficiary of your brother's estate," I opined.

"Yes," Dr. Schultz confirmed. "Melvin had no other family. He never married."

"So he lived in Bethlehem?"

"Yes, and worked here, too, for the past 20 years."

"What did he do for a living?"

"Well, you see, that's one of the reasons I think I am going to need your help. Melvin was ... well he ..."

I thought I had asked a relatively simple question. But experience reminded me there are never simple answers.

"You see," the doctor responded as he took a deep breath, "Melvin always walked to the beat of a different drummer. Actually guitarist, to be exact."

"He was a musician?" I offered.

The doctor paused, then gazed up at the ceiling searching for the right words. He definitely had a story to tell. If and when he spoke, I would not interrupt again.

"Melvin pursued his own agenda even when he was quite young. My father decided long ago when I was seven and Melvin was five that I would ultimately attend medical school, and that Melvin would be an engineer. Right or wrong, I did as I was told, but Melvin would have none of it. One day he found an old guitar, and started playing every waking moment. Music became his life. My father was oblivious to all this. Later, when Melvin graduated from high school, Dad sent him here to Bethlehem to attend Lehigh University to learn how to build bridges. Melvin lasted about two weeks before he dropped out. But instead of returning to Ohio to face the anger of my father, Melvin got a job at a record store near the steel plant. When the owner retired, Melvin began buying into the business. About 10 years ago, he became the owner outright."

The man sitting across from me studied people's feet for a living. I hesitated to ask this next question:

"Owning a record store doesn't sound so unusual. What gives?"

"Do you ever buy CDs?" the doctor asked.

"Certainly. I love music."

"Have you ever been to my brother's place? It's called the Record Riot?"

"Can't say that I have. I usually buy CDs online."

"A wise decision. You see, only the fringe element

shops at my brother's store."

"I'm not following," I interjected.

"I'll put it this way," he said. "Most customers are like you. They buy through the mail, or go to some huge discount store, grab a few CDs, and leave in 10 minutes. My brother focused in on a different market - the connoisseur who wants to analyze every note of every song on each CD. Some dedicated souls have been known to graze in his store like cattle, studying the inventory, for the better part of the day before making a single purchase. He actually encouraged these people, and would talk to them for hours about music and the artists producing the music."

"How are you so familiar with the operation?" I inquired.

"One year my brother was recuperating from surgery and I worked the store for him over Black Friday weekend. This place defines 'ship of fools.' Not that the people aren't nice. They are. But trust me, only a nut would spend the day in a music store. If I wanted to deal with weirdos all day, I would have gone into psychiatric medicine."

"Now, Doctor, don't you think you may be exaggerating the situation a degree or two?" I admonished.

"Listen, counselor, I've got to fly back to Akron tomorrow. I've put too many sore feet on hold as it is. Bunions wait for no one. Here's what I want you to do: take charge of my brother's estate. The only asset is this record store. Figure out what to do with it. Maybe it should be sold; maybe the kids who are running it now can keep it going. Here's the key to the front door."

The doctor reached into his black bag again and placed a dented key on my conference room table.

I love a challenge. We shook hands and I accepted both the key and representation of the estate. I would visit the business the very next morning.

- - - - - - - - - - - - - - - - - - - -

As I approached Fourth and New Streets, I wondered

why, despite my life-long residence in Bethlehem, I had never taken notice of this modest emporium. Probably because it was located within a block of Lehigh University. I must have assumed the Record Riot was just another student hangout clustered within the shadow of the sprawling university campus.

The store's exterior was unremarkable. No hip avant-garde artsy design. Just a tired, weather-worn painted sign located above the entrance with the shop's outdated name. There was a glass door, upon which were pasted a myriad of faded colored posters bearing the illogical names of various musical groups.

The shop resembled a large shoe box, one level, about 3,000 square feet. A far cry from those gigantic super-plexes in which customers get lost in aisle 18. It was just another struggling independent, kept alive solely by the local clientele.

No need for the doctor's dented key. The lights were on, and the disco ball was spinning. It was 10 a.m. and the loud thump thump of music could be heard pulsating from within. Diana Ross was belting out "Stop! In the Name of Love" from six ceiling-mounted speakers.

Chest-high CD racks stood aligned in patient rows, holding thousands of recordings. Surprisingly, unlike the outside of the store, the inside was well-stocked, bright, clean and inviting. The CDs were all categorized alphabetically by type of music and name of artist. I was impressed.

Three people, with name tags attached to chains slung around their necks, labored among the inventory repositioning misplaced CDs incorrectly filed by sloppy, uncaring customers. The name tags were the only proof they were employees, for there was certainly no uniform. As they worked, I realized that these teenagers were, perhaps unknowingly, dancing in synchronization to Diana Ross as her heart-sick voice continued to explain why love had done her wrong. *Stop!* And the three employees froze rigidly in their tracks, until the next phrase - *In the name of love ...*

again filled the air.

Diana Ross faded away just as the Righteous Brothers began to sing. The three employees were now tapping their feet together at different locations of the store as they began to cry out in disorganized unison *You've lost that loving feeling.*

I looked about at the clusters of confusion displayed upon every square foot of each wall. Posters of rock groups past, announcements of concerts yet to take place, and photographs of barely dressed teen idols graced the four corners of the store. And there were several pronouncements, written store policies, and other essential bits of information that covered the counters and cash registers. The large warning posted next to a picture of three naked dwarfs wearing nothing but a limited amount of strategically placed soap bubbles caught my attention:

> *The parental advisory*
> *is a notice to parents*
> *that recordings identified*
> *by this logo may contain*
> *strong language or*
> *depictions of violence,*
> *sex or substance abuse.*
> *Parental discretion is advised.*

Had this foreboding admonition ended with the above language, it might have made some sense. But another sentence followed:

> *This store reserves the right to*
> *restrict sales to children of product*
> *carrying the parental advisory.*

A young lass, perhaps all of 11 years, approached the sales counter, her excited fingers grasping the only CD that could finally make her mundane and incomplete life whole.

"Billy," if the name tag was to be believed, perceived

that a sale was imminent and stopped singing long enough to walk behind the counter where only employees dared tread. He looked down upon this slender girl with the uplifted freckled face, a blushing innocent dressed in a plaid parochial school uniform. Although Billy was but seven years her elder, the difference in their appearances and station in life could well have spanned a millennium.

Billy was no doubt in mourning. He wore black socks, black pants, a black belt, and a black shirt unceremoniously cut off at the armpits. All of it - the boots, the belt, the pants, and shirt were riveted with shiny silver studs up one side and down the next. The back of the shirt announced in uneven lettering: *PUNKS NOT DEAD*. No apostrophe needed.

But it wasn't his back-in-black fashion statement that held my attention. It wasn't the box of cigarettes rolled up and discreetly hidden in the remaining fabric of his torn shirt sleeve. Nor was it that he was 6-feet tall and weighed less than 100 pounds. Rather, it was his hair. Like all faithful students of the punk era gone by, one day he woke up and decided to do it. He shaved his head bald, but for the center one inch of his scalp, extending from the back of his neck to the top of his forehead. His remaining hair was 8 inches long, and had been dyed flourescent red. It had then been waxed and sculpted into 10 spikes.

I couldn't resist. "Are the spikes destroyed nightly when you sleep?"

"Nope," Billy responded matter-of-factly. "I sleep on my side.

Billy was about to ring up the 11-year-old clutching her precious CD. That's when he spotted the parental warning on the CD's cover.

"You're not allowed to buy this," Billy and his hair proclaimed.

"Well ... why not?" the child stammered. A tear welled up in her eye.

"This here CD's got the Parental Advisory, kid. That means there's dirty words or violence on it, so you can only buy it if you got a parent here to advise you. Is your parent here?"

"No."

"Then you got to be 18."

"Can't you make an exception," the disheartened schoolgirl pleaded. "I promise I won't listen to it - it's a birthday present for ... for my younger sister."

Billy hesitated, but her logic failed to persuade the heartless clerk, who took the priceless CD, and placed it under the sales counter.

"Come back in seven years," he suggested.

The solemn child slowly walked out staring at the floor.

As Billy's dejected victim left, another customer cautiously approached, as if she were about to step on an active landmine. She was around 60-years-old, yet she hesitated similar to a teenager buying his first box of prophylactics at the corner drugstore.

"Pardon me," she whispered as she stared at the door. "Could you tell me where the Ls are?"

"The what, lady?"

"Musicians whose last names end in *L*."

"Well, they're all over the store, Ma'am. Each category has musicians with last names ending in an *L*, from jazz to rock to hip-hop. You looking for anyone in particular?"

"Well yes," she confided.

"I can help you if you give me the name," Billy assured. The lady looked left, then right. She lowered her voice even more.

"I'm looking for ... "
She looked about again "... *Liberace*."

There. She did it. The cat was out of the bag. It was like telling the doctor's receptionist that you have hemorrhoids.

Billy didn't flinch. He didn't flinch because he had never heard of the artist.

"Liver-archie? Is that what you said? What is his

newest recording?" a confused Billy inquired.

"No. It's *Liberace*, with a B. You know, the pianist?" she stammered.

Billy scanned the sales floor for his co-worker, Samantha, the part-time college student with the thick glasses and bubble gum pink hair. Hair seemed to be key to the music set.

"HEY, SAMANTHA," Billy screamed above the strains of the overhead music, "WHERE'S LIVER-ARCHIE?"

Five other customers suddenly looked up and shot stares in the woman's direction, even though Billy's skull tattoos were in plain view and generally commanded more attention.

"Now look what you've done!" the embarrassed patron exclaimed, not unlike the wicked witch after Dorothy had thrown a bucket of water on her. And like the witch, unable to withstand any more, she melted away out the door.

"What did I do?" he asked a young man in a shirt and tie who had come out of the back office - the private retail inner sanctum. This must be the manager.

"*Liberace*", the manager corrected his subordinate. "He was a pianist. He's in the Easy Listening section."

"He is?" Billy asked.

"Type in ISBN #8977-63842-27" he instructed.

Billy did as he was told. Liberace's name, as well as his recordings in store inventory, instantly danced in the computer screen reflection displayed in Billy's glasses. Billy appeared unimpressed, but now understood that Liberace was, indeed, a musician, and thanked the manager for the clarification.

I, on the other hand, was dumbstruck. There were probably 10,000 CDs in this store - maybe more. Did the manager know the individual 11-digit number assigned to each CD housed in the store? Did he know the name of each CD and its artist, and its location?

I introduced myself, and explained that I represented the Melvin Schultz estate. The manager shook my hand.

"Hi, I'm George," he advised me. "I've been waiting to hear from you."

I reached for the nearest CD. It was a compilation of Italian love songs by Jerry Vale. On the back was a unique 11- digit code.

"Do you know the code for *this* CD?" I asked George incredulously.

The young man's enormous black eyes turned to a smile.

"*It's 3499-68821-2,*" came the unhesitating answer.

He was right. I moved to an unrelated rack of albums. I indiscriminately reached for another CD - *Ricky Nelson's Greatest Hits.* I studied the 11-digit number. George didn't wait for the question.

"*7284-39446-2.*"

Who was this guy? An idiot savant? Last month my area code changed again. I could no longer remember my own phone number.

"I wouldn't be so impressed," George explained. "Actually, there's nothing to it. You see, the record industry assigns identification numbers to each artist, manufacturer, and type of music. With time, you get to know them."

I was about to pursue the point further, but just then a senior citizen blew through the door. She proceeded to the counter with as much due diligence as her 80-year-old legs would permit.

"You work here, Bub?" she asked me as she peered through peach-framed glasses decorated with aqua-blue sequins. I didn't answer quickly enough.

"Good," she exclaimed. "It's my granddaughter's birthday today, and the party starts in a half hour. She wants *that* new hit song as her birthday gift. Be a dear and get it for me." She gave me a shove with her bony hand.

George and Billy stood motionless for a moment. I looked to them for help. George stepped forward.

"Ma'am?" he asked, "do you know the name of the song, or the album it's on?"

"Who the hell are you?" the blue-hair barked.

"George."

"You work here, too?"

"Sometimes."

"Well, don't just stand there." She pointed in my direction. "Give the older fella here a hand."

"We'll need the name of the song."

"The name? Oh ... yes ... I wrote it on a piece of paper." The frantic customer began to rummage through her worn fake Gucci bag.

"Outa my way," she ordered Billy, as she tipped it upside down onto the sales counter. All of her worldly possessions came hurtling into unwelcomed view.

As the woman continued searching, the back office door to the inner sanctum again swung open. The petite figure of an attractive young woman emerged. George made the introductions.

"This is Heather," he announced. "She is in charge of finding lost songs."

"Thank goodness somebody around here is," the impatient lady sighed as she jammed things back in her bag. "Now be a dear, run along, and go find it," she commanded her new servant. But suddenly we were interrupted.

"You folks sell shoelaces?" We all turned to see a tall man wearing orange sweats. He had approached our little encampment unnoticed. One of his sneakers was missing its laces.

"This is a *record* store," Billy announced dryly. "We don't sell shoelaces."

"I don't see any records," the man observed.

"No," Billy advised him, "just CDs."

"Then my question wasn't so dumb after all, was it?" the man suggested as he walked away.

Dr. Shultz's observations about this store on Black Friday came to mind. But the lady in blue sequins was becoming agitated, so I stood by as Heather returned to the task at hand, facing this AARP member who was now studying her watch.

"Do you recall any words in the title of the song?"

"No, but I think it dealt with love or romance."

"That narrows it down," Heather said. She could now divert her attention away from most of the country songs dealing with warm loyal dogs sitting in dented pick-up trucks.

"Do you know the artist?" Heather asked.

"Somebody with a higher than normal voice," the customer confirmed.

Heather was making substantial progress. The artist was either a pre-pubescent male, the Bee Gees, or female.

"Can you hum the tune?" she suggested.

Some people shouldn't sing in public. To say that the old lady was tone-deaf would have been charitable. But this was *her* 15 minutes. She strode without further encouragement beneath the revolving disco ball, and held her arms out wide.

"Honey," she motioned to Heather, "kill the speakers."

The store grew quiet. Other customers momentarily froze and watched.

Ms. AARP sucked in a deep breath, similar to an anticipatory hippo at the zoo during feeding time, and belted out "Hum a hum hum de waba daba dee do."

"That's the Diaper-Wipes' new single," Heather interjected instantly.

Apparently George was not the only genius on staff.

"Here it is," George chimed in. He walked over to a nearby CD rack, and in a flash located the disc.

I was beginning to understand why this little hole-in-the-wall was still in business. This was no mega-outlet where the customer was cast unassisted and floundering into the recesses of aisle 18. It all had to do with service. They were willing to help, even a Ms. Blue Hair, who was just now finishing her performance. Everyone, employees and customers alike, broke into spontaneous applause.

At that moment, one, no, make that one and a half customers, had just approached the sales counter. A 4-year-old girl, dragging her grandmother by the skirt, had arrived ready to buy. Grandma lifted her toddler up and sat her on the counter.

The child stuck out her pudgy left hand, and presented both a new CD and a juice-stained $20 bill. Thinking back, it wasn't until after I graduated from college that I passed my first twenty. And if memory serves, I used that new found wealth to purchase my first used car. I think I even got some change back with the keys.

Here was a kid who had been on the face of the earth less time than the shoes I was wearing, yet she knew what CD she wanted, and that she had to cough up the cash first. Where had I gone wrong? I couldn't remember the last time one of my clients appeared at my office cash-in-hand.

"Pretty young, don't you think?" I offered.

"She's a bit older than some," George responded. Then he waved me over to a display rack in the rear corner of the store.

"This is our pre-natal section," he announced. Once I realized he was serious, I stared in disbelief. There were such choices as *Mozart For The Embryo, Brahms For The Not Yet Born,* and *Chopin For Your Fetus,* just to name a few.

"We have special speakers over here," George confirmed. "The mother-to-be attaches them to her belly, and the music lover in utero gets an early taste of classical music."

"Want to see the office?" Heather inquired. They led me into the ominous back room. I had entered a repository rarely seen by the shopping public. Thousands of CDs lay stacked in neat piles against every wall, floor to ceiling. It was the Fort Knox of music.

"We inventory and price the CDs here before they go out on the floor," Heather explained.

"And this is where we review all new music."

No wonder she was conversant with the Diaper-Wipes. They weren't her style, but she still listened so she'd be up-to-date for those hard-to-please grandmas who sometimes found their way into the store.

- - - - - - - - - - - - - - - - - - -

It didn't take much to convince Dr. Schultz to sell the business to Heather and George. He agreed to receive a check each month for 15 years. I began buying my CDs at the store as well. Sure, I could have saved some money by purchasing my selections through the mail, but then I would have missed the impromptu live shows.

CHAPTER FIFTEEN:
THE INTERNATIONAL ACQUISITION
OF REAL ESTATE

There is a concept in metaphysics known as the Transmittal Theory, and it goes something like this: there is a finite quantity of happiness and sadness for distribution upon the face of the earth. If someone achieves a degree of happiness, it comes at the expense of someone else who experiences an equal degree of sadness.

Elmer Freihoffer was waiting in my conference room again. He was irritated. Elmer was usually upset about something and he expected me to jump through hoops whenever he showed up at my office. Like the time his neighbor's 14-ounce Chihuahua trespassed on his front lawn and, arguably, had taken liberties with Elmer's favorite rosebush. For a moment, I thought about asking if Elmer had kept any evidence of the corpus depoopus, but that would have gone over his head like a 747 at 35,000 feet.

Elmer was a seasoned practitioner of the Transmittal Theory. At the conclusion of our meeting, in all likelihood, he would feel less irritable and I, in turn, would have a migraine. As a result, Elmer found our little get togethers to be therapeutic, at least, even if I didn't always solve his problems.

"Hello, Elmer ... " I cautiously greeted him.

"This here is the story," he started in as he drummed his fingers on the table. "Remember that 10-acre tract of land I own above the knoll in Longswamp Township?"

"Yes," I confirmed as I pulled out a chair and placed

my notepad and aspirin in front of me.

"Well, I'm dumping it. It's doing me no good. The real money is in residential housing. Last week, I went to the township zoning guy. It was my intent to subdivide the land. When I did the math, it looked like I'd have to create 20 half-acre lots. That way, I'd have enough money to extend water and sewer lines. But the zoning guy claims the land is in the *agricultural zoning district,* and that the minimum area per lot is five acres. That means I can only create two lots. Two lots! Where's the damn money in that?"

I turned toward the bookshelf and reached for my copies of the local zoning ordinances. As I did, Elmer gave me a 30- second lesson in politics, civics, economics, and the law.

"This is America, right? Land of the so-called free? I've been paying taxes on that tract for over 15 years. It's my land, damn it. If I want to sell off housing sites, that's nobody else's business. I should be able to make a profit just like the next guy."

I had in minutes located the Longswamp Township zoning ordinance, and began to peruse the minimum lot size requirements within the agricultural zone.

"Looks like the zoning administrator gave you correct data. Lots up there must contain at least five acres in area. The township is probably trying to maintain an 'open space' policy that restricts development and keeps the farms intact." My explanation didn't sit well.

"What the hell ever happened to free enterprise? You know who's to blame? I'll tell you who's to blame. Politicians and lawyers. That's who. Too many stinkin' laws in this country, and too many people enforcing them."

Elmer pounded his fist on the table, just as the first twinges of a migraine crept up the back of my neck.

Ironically, Elmer was in the road paving business, yet never once did I blame him for potholes. They existed, and as a result, he made an adequate living. Same with zoning ordinances, and the law in general. Statutes exist, and because of them, I make an adequate living. It wasn't my fault if, once in a while, someone was ensnared by one. Just like a pothole, there were remedies.

"You could petition to have your zoning district changed," I suggested.

"Time and money," he protested.

Elmer was right. Whether fixing potholes or researching the law, the process was always costly. At least now he felt better. I, on the other hand, began to pour a glass of water and reach for the aspirin bottle.

Had Elmer's real estate been located in the Canadian Yukon Territory, in all probability, the lack of both lawyers and law there would have permitted him to proceed uninterrupted with his proposed housing subdivision. I know this for a fact, since I used to own part of a subdivision there myself.

- - - - - - - - - - - - - - - - - - -

It was 1955. My parents had just purchased their first TV. I sat transfixed in front of the 7-inch black and white screen, watching blurry cartoon characters dance before my amazed eyes. Then, without realizing it, a life-altering event took place: I witnessed my first TV advertisement. The dancing cartoons disappeared, and in their place magically stood Futzo the Clown. He had a big red nose and bigger shoes. I sat 10 inches from the screen, mesmerized.

"Hey kids! It's time for the Sally Starr Show, with your favorite cowgirl, Sally Starr, and her trail-blazing sidekick, Chief Halftown."

I was seven. I had never blazed a trail. I didn't have a sidekick. What the hell was this clown, standing somewhere in a Philadelphia sound studio, jabbering about?

"But first - do you know what's the best tasting cereal in the whole wide world? That's right! It's Quaker Puffed Rice - wholesome nuggets of goodness shot from guns."

I instantly wondered what caliber of food was processed by the discharge of a weapon. Frantic Futzo continued his pitch.

"I eat Quaker Puffed Rice every morning because it tastes sooo very good. So next time you're at the store with Mom, tell her you want a box of Quaker Puffed Rice, too!"

I was riveted, but skeptical. After all, scores of radio sales pitches touted products like Rice Krispies and Sugar Frosted Flakes. I loved the former because when I placed my ear really close, they did, indeed, go *snap, crackle, and pop*. And I partook of the latter because Tony the Tiger said they were G-R-E-A-T, and he enjoyed an unsullied reputation for veracity.

Futzo wasn't quite finished, though. "And   kids, guess what you'll find inside?"

Even at 7, I had never been impressed with the useless toys and gadgets companies invariably stuck in their food containers as an incentive to purchase the product. Who needed a secret decoder ring that shot signals all the way to Jupiter anyway? The way I saw it, if they were giving it away, I didn't want it, even if it did glow in the dark.

And then Futzo brought it home.

"You also get a deed to one square inch of land in the Canadian Yukon Territory!"

"What's a deed?" I yelled to Mom as she fixed dinner in the kitchen.

"Well son, there are good deeds and bad deeds. When you do a good deed, you go to heaven, and when you do a bad deed -"

"Mom!"

"Yes?"

"Not *that* kind of deed. A deed to the Canadian Yukon Territory."

Mom put down her paring knife, and came in and listened to the tail end of the commercial. I soon learned that I could own land where a gold rush had taken place. Things were starting to get interesting.

"Can we buy a box of Quaker Puffed Rice?" I asked.

"You mean you're willing to give up Rice Krispies

and Sugar Frosted Flakes?"

"Well, they're boring. And besides I think it's time I owned some land."

Mom played along. She agreed to switch if I promised to finish the box down to the very last puff of rice - whether I liked it or not.

That Saturday afternoon we went grocery shopping. I ran to the cereal aisle. Futzo may have just been a clown, but his information on the Canadian wilderness was on target. I gingerly held a box of Puffed Rice, the front cover of which announced that inside reposed the legal documentation that would transfer ownership of a single square inch of real estate from the present title holder in the Yukon, to a 7-year-old boy who lived in Pennsylvania.

I cradled the box in my arms as we drove home in our yellow Kaiser coupe. Then I ran into the house.

"I'm having Puffed Rice for dinner," I announced, as I ripped open the lid of the box. I dug my hand into the depths of the weightless puffs. Left side. Right side. Finally I felt a large piece of paper sealed in plastic wrap and delicately slid it out. I studied the document in awe. It had big words. Mom read the preamble:

> *This Indenture, made the 4th day of January, in the year of Our Lord One Thousand Nine Hundred and Fifty-five between Klondike Big Inch Land Co., Inc., a body corporate duly registered for the purpose of carrying on business in the Yukon Territory, having its head office for the said Territory in the city of Whitehorse, hereinafter called the "Grantor" of the first part and*

—————————————————————

(fill in your name)

"Should I print or write my name?" I inquired.
"You should write it."
I had never executed my signature on a legal

document before. I was about to learn more in the next five minutes then I would during the first year of law school.

"Do you have a pencil?" I asked Mom.

"You should use a pen."

"Why?"

"So no one can erase your name and insert his."

"Why would anyone do that?"

"To steal the land."

"Do you have a pen?"

"Yes. Here it is."

"Do I put *Larry* first, or *Fox*?"

"This is a legal document, so you should use your legal name, *Lawrence*."

That made sense. My legal name had the word LAW in it, so I now understood why it was my legal name. I wrote it on the deed.

"Well, what else does the deed say?" I inquired. Mom read the next paragraph.

All and singular that certain parcel or tract of land and premises situate lying and being in the Yukon Territory more particularly known and described as follows: Tract Numbered L 425916 comprising by admeasurement one square inch more or less as more particularly described in that certain subdivision plan, prepared and acknowledged by the Grantor under date the 15th day of December, A.D. 1954 and deposited at the registered office of the Grantor in the Yukon Territory of the whole of Lot two hundred forty-three (243) in Group Two (2) in Yukon territory, as said lot is shown on a plan of survey of record in the Legal Surveys and Aeronautical Charts Division of the Department of Mines and Technical Surveys at Ottawa under number 6718, containing by admeasurement Nineteen and eleven hundredths (19.11) acres more or less; together with all and singular the easements, hereditaments and appurtenances to the same belonging or in any way appertaining with reversion and reversions, remainder and remainders, rents, issues and profits thereof and all the estate, right, title, interest, claim, property and demand both at law and in equity of the said Grantor of, in, to or out of the same or any part thereof.

This wording took up three square inches of fine print.

"What does all that mean?" I asked.

"You own part of Canada, dear."

"Neat. Where?"

"Northwest of here in the Yukon."

"When can we visit my land?"

"Check with your father, dear. He plans the family trips."

During the next five weeks, I ate Quaker Puffed Rice for breakfast, lunch, and dinner. I ate the stuff for snacks at night. I had never been so regular. Soon I possessed five whole square inches of land, and an extreme distaste for Quakers and their damned rice. But it didn't matter. The advertising campaign had come to its conclusion, and all transfer of land had ceased.

Now that I owned part of a subdivision, it was time to design my dream home to be constructed in the Yukon. Because I held title to just five square inches of land, the foundation of the residence could consist of but a five square inch pole, with the house resting on a platform situated on top. I drew the design myself:

The concept, of course, was flawed. I had failed to realize that in all likelihood, the five deeds of land weren't adjoining. I might have to build five smaller houses on five separate poles.

Now that I think back, the idea was sheer marketing genius. Someone found a place in the Yukon where subdivision in any form or size was permissible, and then tied those deeds together with the sale of Puffed Rice. Even if this genius had purchased and subdivided just a single acre of land, it may have been more than enough. There are 43,560 square feet in a square acre, and each square foot has 144 square inches. In other words, a square acre of land can be partitioned into 6,272,640 square inches. That's a lot of boxes of cereal.

A few years ago, I was rummaging through an old desk drawer. Much to my astonishment, I found five faded deeds. I decided to check up on my real estate investment. The next day, I called the Provincial Headquarters of the Yukon Territory, and ultimately spoke with the Royal Office of the Deeds Registry. To my sorrow, I was advised that because I, and several other millions of Puffed Rice consumers had failed to pay real estate taxes when due, our ownership rights had lapsed, and the subdivision had been forfeited to the Crown. If only I had been advised that the taxes were due, I would have obtained a loan from my parents, and paid the levy.

My international real estate investment had proven to be valueless - or was it?

Shortly after I found my deeds, I learned that some nut on the Internet had been running an advertisement seeking to buy the old cereal deeds. Last time I looked, he was offering a couple hundred dollars a pop. I guess he still wants to build his dream house in the Yukon. Actually, the price he's proposing is probably a little low. After all, in 1955, a box of Puffed Rice cost about $.45. If I had put that sum in an interest-bearing bank account back in 1955, today I'd have more than a million dollars.

Still, there's a lesson to be learned about the value of

a wise investment in land. As an economics professor once explained to me: If you had a gold dollar in the year 1788, you could buy an acre of land in Pennsylvania. Today, if you had that very same gold dollar, you could still purchase the same acre of land.

CHAPTER SIXTEEN:
THE INVOCATION

The "Blessing Of The Fleet" occurred annually at the start of the fishing season. The handsome Catholic priest stood on the dock of Coast Guard Station Atlantic City, where God could easily see him, and as the fishing vessels passed by, he asked for His divine protection, just as a fisherman from Galilee might have done two millennia before him. The ceremony always generated a feeling of security, since the priest also remembered to say a prayer over each Coast Guard boat moored at the dock - sea-going rescue ships in which we, enlisted personnel, placed our lives.

This very same priest also blessed parishioners, and when the Spirit moved him, their pets. On the day set aside for "The Blessing of the Animals," the priest invited his flock to Our Lady by the Sea Church, where he requested that God's grace protect each descendant from Noah's Ark. The ceremony was always well attended, predominantly by little children, who brought the expected animated dogs and bored cats. But other pets arrived, too, and they also were the objects of the invocation. There were birds, and lizards, and rabbits, and snakes, and turtles, and guinea pigs, and frogs, all presented in the outstretched protective hands of their masters. And all were blessed, using the same power as had been directed upon the passing fleet. Not a canary, nor a goldfish was missed by the gentle priest, who never seemed to exhaust either his patience, or his supply of blessings. Was there one left for me, too?

Rudy and Alverta Gerber had been operating the ice cream shop on High Street for almost 30 years. Selling frozen desserts had not made them wealthy, but they had managed to put two children through college, and to keep a roof over their heads. It was time to retire, to some place warm, and so they listed the business for sale. It didn't take long for a willing buyer to come along. Their business was profitable and in a good location.

Kamal Patel, an engineer with a physics background, had just accepted a golden parachute from his Fortune 500 company in the industrial park off Westgate Drive, and at age 50, felt there was more to life besides playing golf and mowing the lawn. He and his wife, Shakuntala, a nurse, yearned for a change. They wanted to be employers - not employees - in control of their own destiny. The ice cream shop looked like the answer.

Rudy and Alverta asked me to draft an agreement of sale and stopped into my office to review the paperwork. We had known each other for more than three decades. I watched their children grow up.

"It looks good to me," Rudy said. "I think you've covered all the key points we discussed last week."

"Good," I responded.

"There's just one thing," Mrs. Gerber noted. "These buyers immigrated from India. I hope they get up to speed quickly on the ice cream business. It's not as easy as it looks."

"We've agreed to stay on as consultants for one month after the purchase," Rudy assured me, "but I still can't help but wonder if they know what it's going to be like being self-employed and working 12-hour days."

A week later, settlement occurred at the law office of Attorney Julius Hunsberger, legal counsel for the buyers. I drove across town with Rudy and Alverta. This would be my first contact with the new buyers. We were ushered by a friendly receptionist into Hunsberger's conference room.

There sat Julius who, because of his arthritis, remained seated. His polite clients, on the other hand, immediately rose from their seats, and greeted us with firm handshakes. Then they introduced the other stranger in the room.

"This is Paranj Brihan," Mr. Patel advised us. "He is the spiritual advisor of our Hindu Temple."

There was little doubt. This was, indeed, a holy man. He wore a simple white turban wrapped about his gray hair, and a full-length white robe. He appeared to have spoken to God every single day. He lowered his head slightly in my direction, so I returned the gesture. Then we all sat down, and Mr. and Mrs. Patel bought the ice cream business - from the front door lock, to the interior stock, and any barrels in between. Mr. and Mrs. Gerber received a certified check representing payment in full, and this brought smiles to their faces. Everyone rose to leave, except Attorney Hunsberger, who still complained of knee pain.

Mr. Patel then spoke. "Of course, you are all invited to our new store for the blessing of the frozen yogurt cultures," he announced.

I had never before attended such a ceremony, and so I accepted the invitation, as did the Gerbers. As Mr. Patel would later explain, the benevolent bacteria that helped produce the yogurt were considered living organisms worthy of God's grace. The blessing occurred in a language foreign to me. But I sensed that I understood the significance of the priest's invocation. Afterward, we all sat down together, and ate some of the bacteria.

CHAPTER SEVENTEEN:
A VISIT TO NEW YORK CITY

It was one of those rolling, angry storms that sweep across eastern Pennsylvania each August. I had just pulled into my mother's driveway as the winds picked up and lightning began to flash in the early evening sky. This system would not pass gently into the night.

Having lived in her house for more than 40 years, Mom knew exactly what to do. She had already begun to light several candles downstairs in preparation for the inevitable loss of power. Back when I was a kid, it seemed *the lights went out* with alarming regularity. I always wrote it off to snow storms, high winds, or heavy rain. Mom said it was thin wires.

No sooner had I rushed through the front door out of the driving rain, when flickering lights announced the expected loss of electricity. I hung my raincoat in the foyer. The living room became enveloped in a warm glow. Two candles on the piano, another on the refrigerator, just like when I was a young boy.

It was quiet, except for the tick tock of the grandfather clock, the pelting of the rain outside, and the occasional roll of thunder. Mom looked forward to our Sunday evening visits, especially since Dad's passing two years earlier. We'd sit and talk, or perhaps I'd fix something around the house. Mom always got tired around 10:00, so we'd say our good-byes, I'd kiss her on the cheek and return home.

I don't recall how the topic came up, but as we sat in

the flickering candlelight, with no TV or radio to interrupt us, I asked Mom what had been the most unusual event in her life. From a self-centered standpoint, I figured she'd unequivocally focus upon the birth of her children, or some other family related event. But as she thought momentarily in the stillness of the dark room, I saw the hint of a mischievous smile overcome her face as she stepped back in time.

"What is it, Mom?"

Age and wisdom go hand-in-hand, and so in Mom's golden years, she was more of a patient listener than a big talker - which was usually fine with me since I always had lots to say and news to share about a new client or a case in which I had recently become involved. But her face. This look of hers. She clearly had a story to tell.

"C'mon, Mom," I urged. "What gives?"

"There's something I've never told you, Larry ... "

It was the tone of her voice. She was suddenly younger, her eyes clear again. A pleasant memory enveloped her.

"The most unusual event in my life ... " she mused. "I think it was when I served as the first United Nations Representative to the Republic of Mozambique."

A lightning bolt struck nearby. Seconds later came the crash of thunder. But it was what Mom had just said that actually caused me to jump.

"I beg your pardon?"

"I suppose I should have said something before, but who would have believed me. And anyway, everyone should have a secret or two. The truth is, I was present to cast the initial vote on behalf of Mozambique when the United Nations first convened."

This observation - or perhaps it was a confession - raised more questions than it answered. I had no idea Mom possessed political ties with Mozambique. How had she hidden her true lineage all these years? Had Dad been in on the secret? Did I have dual citizenship? Was I adopted?

My expression said it all, even in the darkened room,

so Mom drew a deep breath, and sat back in her overstuffed reclining chair. As she did so, her legs were lifted three feet from the floor by the automatic foot support. Thusly situated, she was ready to come clean. I was all ears.

"It disheartened me when the League of Nations failed to achieve world peace," Mom began. "I had hoped that war would be outlawed, and that everyone would start to get along. My hopes were uplifted again when they created the United Nations. It was 1953, and you kids were still really small. Just like any other mother, I wanted you to grow up in a peaceful world. The United Nations sounded like the answer to my prayers, so when I heard the opening ceremonies were taking place just 80 miles away in New York City, I went. After Dad left for work, I gave you kids to Aunt Bert for the day and hopped on a bus into the city."

My mother was sincere about her life-long quest for peace. And she was also motivated by an unending curiosity to witness life first hand. Sitting in front of the television to garner world news was to her just a second rate way of getting hearsay from a stranger. Wherever the action was, she was there. She attended most of our local city council meetings. She often dragged me to debates regarding national issues sponsored by the local colleges. Her voracious quest to become involved sprang from an impoverished childhood.

She had grown up in Boston, during the Great Depression. Her family was desperately poor. Sometimes for dinner they would huddle together and eat lard sandwiches - two pieces of day-old bread smeared with grease. The Depression impacted the rest of her life. She kept quantities of cash in hidden odd locations just in case the banks crashed. And during my entire youth as a resident in her home, not once did I ever get to eat a yellow banana. "Eat the dark ones first," she'd insist, "before they go bad."

"It was August, 1953, a beautiful Monday morning. I took the 10 o'clock bus. First was the Port Authority. Then I took another bus cross-town to the new United Nations building. Some guys were still sweeping construction debris out front. It had just been completed and it was awe-inspiring. They were having opening day ceremonies, so I decided to attend, like when I watch the city council meetings. The line to get in stretched for two city blocks. That was too long for me, so I took a walk around to the back of the building, to look for another door. I found one in the rear. There were only about a thousand people waiting to get in, and the line was moving at a pretty good pace. In less than 15 minutes, I was up to the guard at the door. He asked me something - I think it was in French - about diplomatic identification, so I showed him my library card. Back in those days, there weren't any metal detectors or other security stuff. People trusted you. He waved me in.

"Well, I followed the crowd, and soon we entered the General Assembly chamber. Most of the seats were taken. Then I noticed the delegation from Mozambique had failed to arrive, which made sense - do you have any idea how far Mozambique is from New York?"

I was dumbstruck.

"Mom! You didn't! Didn't you realize you had entered the U.N. with all of the world's diplomats?"

"I guess I should have. After all, some of them were in turbans and kimonos. But it was New York, so I didn't want to stare or I'd look out of place myself. Well anyway, I sat down at Mozambique, and was soon discussing the general state of affairs with this guy from Mauritania. In moments Dag Hammarskjold called the meeting to order. The first vote was to accept the new United Nations charter. So on behalf of Mozambique, I did. The vote was almost unanimous, which makes sense. Why would someone travel half way around the world just to say his country wasn't interested in the charter?

Anyway, that's it in a nutshell. The most unusual event in my life. I attended a fancy diplomatic party that followed, but left just in time to get the 4:50 p.m. bus back home. Then I made dinner. Then your Dad came home."

I didn't doubt her story for a second. But I wondered ... had she retained some token or souvenir of her international experience?

"They took our picture at the opening day ceremony," Mom said.

My heart stopped. "Do you have the photograph?"

"Not exactly. I didn't stay long enough to get one of the autographed originals. But I can show you a copy."

Mom tilted her recliner back to the floor, and rose slowly from the thick cushion. Bookshelves spanned the entire south wall of the living room. There sat her treasured eclectic collection of seemingly unrelated books and manuscripts gathered during 75 years of life. My father's books remained separate and undisturbed along the north wall. Without hesitation and in spite of the dim candlelight, Mom effortlessly located her only volume of the Encyclopedia Britannica. It was the 1953 "U" treatise.

She paged to the United Nations entry, a narrative with a large photo of the General Assembly. She handed me the book. The highlighted caption of the photograph read "Convening of Opening Day Ceremonies in the General Assembly." Hundreds of delegates stood facing the camera. The names of each country represented were positioned at each seat. Mom was in the front row, the only delegate from Mozambique. She was flashing a broad *Alfred E. Newman What Me Worry?* smile.

"They had the shorter delegates without the turbans take a position down in the front," Mom recalled. "It's a nice picture, don't you think?"

CHAPTER EIGHTEEN:
THE SINISTER COMMODE

There is little in my life that I have found more challenging or satisfying than the study of Latin. Its derivations, declensions, and conjugations unlock the secrets of all Romance languages, and by doing so, lend a greater insight into the art of communication in the English language. Consider, as but one example, the English word "sincere," which has been defined as meaning "free from deceit" or "unadulterated." This word arises from the combination of two unrelated Latin words: "sine," meaning "without," and "cera," meaning "wax." In ancient Rome, that which was "without wax" was "free from deceit." Specifically, when wooden furniture was constructed or repaired, if a crack or scratch were found, some unscrupulous merchants would cover the defect by rubbing colored wax into the imperfection in an attempt to conceal it. Furniture that was not fraudulently treated was considered to be unadulterated, and thus of higher quality.

The English words "sinister" and "dexterous" boast an interesting history. In Latin, the word for "left" is "sinistra," and the word for "right" is "dexter." For centuries, use of the left hand was considered to be sinister, and as a result, many left-handed students were forced to learn to write with their proper "dexterous" hand.

- - - - - - - - - - - - - - - - - - -

I served as solicitor to the Building Code Appeals

Board of Hamilton Township.   Whenever the township building inspector found a construction code violation, or a deviation from the fire or safety ordinance, the owner of the offending structure faced one of two options: either correct the problem, or seek a waiver of the regulation from the Building Code Appeals Board.

Colonial Enterprises Inc. was in the process of completing the final stages of its 600,000 square foot office and commercial complex. The 12-story edifice possessed 85 office suites, two cafeterias, an atrium, four elevators, and parking for more than 600 vehicles. It had taken three years to design and construct the project, but the effort was about to pay off. Over 90 percent of the suites had already been rented to future tenants.   The only thing precluding habitation of the structure was a final inspection by the township, followed by issuance of the official occupancy permit.   The township inspector was requested by the contractor to complete his evaluation so that 70 or 80 anxious corporate tenants might move in during the next two weeks. The inspection was Thursday. I received a fax on Friday.   The one paragraph message, written to me by Inspector Griffith, effectively halted more than 50 fully-loaded moving vans from delivering thousands of desks, filing cabinets, and computers.

> *Dear Attorney Fox:*
> *My final inspection of the Colonial Enterprises Complex has revealed that toilets installed during this last month are equipped with non-conforming handles. Occupancy permit cannot be issued. Please advise.*
>
> > *Sincerely,*
> > *C. H. Griffith,*
> > *Township Inspector*

It was a copy of this missive, remitted to the sub-contractor in charge of plumbing supplies, that occasioned a frantic call to my office.

"Mr. Poindexter is calling," my secretary informed me. "He says it's an emergency."

I had not yet read the fax, as I was temporarily detained in my office bathroom.

"Who is he? What file is he calling about?" I shouted from behind closed doors.

"Toilets," she hollered.

"Tell him we don't need any. We have plenty."

"I think it deals with a fax I just put on your desk."

I emerged from my temporary seclusion earlier than scheduled and stumbled for the phone. "Hello, this is Larry Fox."

"This is Milton Poindexter," a distraught voice announced.

"How may I help you?"

"It's your township building code inspector - he's holding up our occupancy permit. He claims the toilet handles need to be on the right, not the left, but no one said anything to me when I ordered *lefties* and now they're installed, and the tenants can't move in, and the leases are supposed to start next week, and the moving vans are ready to roll, and - "

"Excuse me, sir," I interrupted, fearful Poindexter might never come up for air. "What file are you calling about?"

That question seemed to catch the hysterical plumber by surprise. He had to think for a moment. "It's Colonial something. Colonial Enterprises. No one ever said I couldn't put flushers on the left."

I now knew less than when the conversation had started. I told Poindexter I'd get back to him just as soon as I had flushed out all the facts. I called the township building inspector for a more dispassionate explanation. Inspector Griffith was very capable and quickly detailed the problem.

"The National Building Code requires that handicapped accessible toilets maintain the handle on the right. Colonial installed them on the left. If they want a variance or waiver, they'll need to petition the Township

Building Code Appeals Board."

A hearing was scheduled the very next week. Colonial brought its attorney, architect, contractor, sub-contractor, and a stenographer. After all, each day's delay was, conservatively, costing the owner more than $100,000 in lost rentals. This army of concerned witnesses appeared before the board, which was composed of the township fire inspector, building code inspector, zoning administrator, and the plumbing inspector. I hoped and prayed there wouldn't be too many technical questions thrown my way, since what I knew about this form of privity of contract had, for the most part, been learned on the john.

Mortimer Piper, counsel for Colonial, and presumably an expert on the law of commodes, offered to outline the issues for consideration by the board. I have always been wary of experts. The prefix "ex" is derived from Latin, and means "from." "Pert" comes from the English "spurt," and describes a "drip under pressure." Enough said. Mortimer dove right in.

"You see, the Colonial tower design, pursuant to state regulation, provides one toilet for every 12 occupants. Therefore, there are 360 toilets, of which one third, or 120 are "Americans with Disabilities Act" compliant for wheelchair and similar accessibility. The new State Building Code requires flushing handles to be installed on the right side of the commode since most folks are not ambidextrous and prefer not to flush from the left. Our fixtures are on the left, a problem no one seems to have noticed until the final inspection."

"What's the cost to correct the problem?" Zoning Administrator Rodney Perch inquired.

"About $1,300 per toilet," Piper estimated. "The cost is significant, since each toilet is operated by an individual automotic pressure-flushing mechanism that evacuates and refills the commode in approximately one-half second. Reinstalling the flushing mechanism on the right side would require a retro-fitting ab initio."

As a student of Latin, I knew just what he meant.

Retro-fitting a commode ab initio would certainly not be easy. These were the new type of toilet which, when activated, produced an instantaneous and startling flush.

Quite frankly, I'm not so sure that such a design is much of an improvement over the old *10-second swirl-a-glug-glug* method. I can still recall one horrifying moment when, as I stood to pull up my pants, my wallet fell in. Realizing what had happened, I had more than ample time to reclaim all of my worldly possessions, as they circulated about, similar to a ball bouncing around a roulette wheel. Such would certainly not have been the case had this tragedy occurred with one of the new Colonial toilets. With their over-designed fixtures, the user wouldn't have had a chance. In less time than it takes to say *two-ply*, the victim's wallet would have been half way to Hong Kong. What's more, depending on the toilet posture at time of flushing, the user could have lost more than just his wallet.

Attorney Piper presented a well-reasoned argument as to why the handles ought to remain on the left, predicated upon the theory that "possession is nine tenths of the law." I was growing more confused by the moment. How does one actually determine the left or right of a toilet? Is it when facing the commode, or when sitting thereupon? I've used them both ways, even though the gentler half of our population doesn't do so. For them there are formal unwritten rules, such as the nonsensical Always-Put-The-Toilet-Seat-Down edict. Personally, I have never sat on anything unless I've looked first.

Left-handed bathroom discrimination reaches far beyond the mere placement of commode handles. Those of us who are left-handed know only too well the painful discrimination foisted upon us by the manufacturers of trouser zipper flaps. There is no such thing as a left-handed pair of pants - the zipper can only be operated by the right hand. At the very least, clothing should be ambi-zipperous (another Latin term).

It's the *Americans with Disabilities Act* (ADA) legislation that seeks to assure equality among all

Americans. This Act is enforced by the Federal Government, which, remarkably, is the only entity in the nation that is permitted to discriminate. As an example, Congress (the members of which have no mandatory retirement age) has determined that all commercial airline pilots must retire at age 60. This regulation has been upheld by the Supreme Court, which is composed of nine jurists who are permitted to serve for life.

Ultimately it becomes the responsibility of the United States Supreme Court to interpret the *Americans With Disabilities Act*, in an endeavor to eradicate illegal discrimination predicated upon a disability.

We all know the story of Casey Martin, a professional golfer, who sought the assistance of this nation's Highest Court to correct a discriminatory policy illegally foisted upon him by the PGA Tour Inc. Martin suffers from a degenerative circulatory disorder that has caused his right leg to atrophy. As a result, Martin is incapable of walking the entire length of a golf course without suffering severe pain. Therefore, he requested that the PGA permit him to utilize a golf cart during professional tournaments. His request was denied. The PGA rules require at the highest levels of tournament competition that "players shall walk at all times during a stipulated round."

Martin believed this arbitrary pronouncement by the PGA was discriminatory and constituted a violation of Title III of the *Americans with Disabilities Act*. An initial proceeding before the Federal District Court concluded with a decision in his favor. The PGA Tour Inc. then appealed this ruling to the Ninth Circuit Court of Appeals, which similarly found in Martin's favor. The PGA Tour, Inc. then perfected an appeal to the U.S. Supreme Court. Seven of the nine justices of this final tribunal again found in favor of Martin - he may ride a golf cart during professional competition.

Until I studied this case, I had no idea how significantly my own life had been adversely impacted by illegal discrimination. You see, I, too, just like Martin, have always wanted to be a professional athlete. Golf would do, but basketball is more my speed. The reasons are quite simple: I would like to be paid millions of dollars to play a game I enjoy three or four hours every other day for five months, and then relax the rest of the year at my villa in the Bahamas.

However, until Casey Martin put the proverbial golf cart before the course, this would never have been possible, because, you see, I am *vertically challenged.* I find that most basketball hoops are simply too high. Also, I am over 50 now, and so I can't run as fast as I used to. On the other hand, I can still walk, so to a certain degree, I am better off than Mr. Martin.

So here's my proposal to make things a little less discriminatory toward me despite my disabilities: I will be permitted to play in the National Basketball Association (hopefully for the Philadelphia 76ers so I don't have to commute very far from home). Because I am only 5 feet 8 inches tall, and shrinking about a centimeter a year through no fault of my own, I shall have my own basketball hoop installed at *my* eye level, since the 7-foot tall players already have the same advantage. Also, since I can't run as fast as the other players, I'd like to use a golf cart when dribbling up and down the basketball court. If this is not permitted, I plan to sue in Federal District Court.

- - - - - - - - - - - - - - - - - - -

"And so, gentlemen of the Township Building Code Appeals Board, what we seek is permission to keep the toilet handles on the right side of the commode." With those dramatic words, Mortimer Piper, legal counsel for Colonial Enterprises, began his brilliant closing, an argument predicated upon the assertion that equality of bathroom use, or *piddle-parity* as he called it, was never intended by either the drafters of the U.S. Constitution, or the promulgators of the *Americans with Disabilities Act.*

Learned counsel then played the "sex card" and

closed with a dramatic summation.

"A review of the federal legislative history affirms that Congress realized that women require more commodes than do men. For that reason, construction standards for all new stadiums, amphitheaters, and ball parks, mandate that more bathroom facilities be constructed for women than for men. Arguably, this is sexual discrimination. By the same logic, the fact that we have installed more handles on the left than on the right should not delay issuance of the occupancy permit. No one ever said there had to be equality in bathroom accommodations."

Attorney Piper sat down in a heap, exhausted from his emotional oration. Now it was up to the Township Appeals Board to grant either a waiver, or refuse the issuance of an occupancy permit. They huddled together, whispering, like four teenage girls in a high school cafeteria deciding if they should all go to the bathroom together. Males don't typically engage in such after meal toilet-cluster-processions - another reason why the concept of piddle-parity is flawed.

One thing is clear. Were Supreme Court Justice Scalia, who wrote a dissenting opinion in the Martin case, serving on the Township Appeals Board, there would be no mercy. If Casey Martin ought to walk the damn golf course in pain, then some left-handed guy in a wheelchair trying to take a dump better start learning how to flush with his right hand.

CHAPTER NINETEEN:
MY NEW CAR

I drive a "classic car" that pre-dates the Kennedy Administration because that is what I can afford. Sure, I could charge outrageous retainer fees before I accept a new file. But then that would just put an even bigger burden on other lawyers to represent an unfair proportion of the down-and-out souls.

I'm not looking for the reader's pity. Rather, my ownership of a two-tone gray Buick Skyhawk is simply an undeniable fact of life. Betty (I named her) runs well, which is more than I can say about myself.

Last month I drove my Buick to the quarterly bar association meeting at the Hilton Hotel. Scores of lawyers were alighting from their Mercedes, Caddys, and Beemers. As I struggled to exit Betty while attempting to avoid an emerging seat spring, I realized some of my colleagues were staring and muttering to each other. I could read their lips.

"Isn't that a shame. He must not have any paying clients."

"He's been in practice over 30 years. He probably gambled it all away."

"At least we won't have to fight with him for valet parking."

Even some of my clients have politely suggested that a successful attorney ought to drive something with a little more zip.

"You get no respect with that piece of shit," a helpful friend recently advised.

That's not true. Just last week I came to a four-way stop sign, along with a Mercedes, a Cadillac, and a Jaguar. Each of these drivers soon displayed a look of panic as I inched closer to the intersection. They waved me through as if I were in a presidential motorcade.

I bought Betty a few months ago at Bob's Used Cars. I don't patronize car lots where the vehicles are *pre-owned*. They usually cost too much. Bob has been a loyal client of mine for more than 20 years. He knew I'd been looking for a new car for seven or eight years, ever since the transmission on my Desoto began to slip. When the Buick was towed to his lot, he gave me a call.

"You better get over here fast. This one's a real cream-puff," he confided. "It has less than 50,000 miles, and rides like you're sitting in a bucket full of tits. The previous owner only drove it to church on Sundays. As soon as I find a rear axle, some smart shopper will snap it up."

There was no time to lose. My old Desoto, when followed by other traffic, became alarmed and often unexpectedly, perhaps involuntarily, blew a huge cloud of smoke out its rusted tailpipe in an instinctive endeavor to flee from its enemies by subterfuge, similar to an octopus. Had I ever been arrested for speeding, I would have accepted the ticket as a compliment, and framed it on the wall next to my diplomas.

Even though Bob was in the used car business, he could be trusted. His only fault was that he would show up late for appointments. It was always the same excuse. His car broke down.

I dropped what I was doing immediately and hurried over to his showroom - which was merely a pre-owned trailer he picked up at a fire sale. I glanced over the glistening rows of cars in anticipation of locating the Buick. Somewhere out there was my new car waiting patiently to meet me. Bob saw me drive up in a cloud of smoke and met me near the third row of cars. I was standing next to a rusted hulk that might once have been a Plymouth 20 or 30 years ago. The driver's seat had disintegrated. The tires were bald.

Half of the vehicle's roof was missing.

"Who in their right mind would buy this piece of garbage?" I inquired.

"There's an ass for every seat," came Bob's unhesitating answer. "I'll sell that beauty within a week. Now come with me."

I followed him over to the fourth row of vehicles. There sat my new vintage Buick. It was everything I had ever wanted, and more. It had an A.M. radio, two-tone gray paint, a rear view mirror, translucent steering wheel, a seat belt, and matching floor mats.

"I'll take it," I beamed.

Betty has served me well in the practice of law. Not one client who has seen me driving around town has complained about my fees. There is an unspoken presumption that if the Buick is all I can afford, I must not be overcharging. But that's not the motivation behind driving my new old car. I simply refuse to pay monthly car loan installments exceeding the amount of my home mortgage. And who actually needs all those fancy extras and gadgets they stick on new cars? If you rode around blindfolded in Betty, aside of the rotting upholstery smell, you wouldn't be able to tell if you were sitting in a Rolls Royce or a Buick, unless you asked for air conditioning. And frankly, you can get *that* by rolling down one of the hand-crank windows.

- - - - - - - - - - - - - - - - - - -

Stanley Przylutsky was waiting in my office conference room. My receptionist had failed to warn me of his advanced state of agitation.

"Get this, Larry. I bought a new Jaguar last month, right? So the wife says she needs a quart of milk. So yesterday I went over to the grocery store at the 7th Street Mall."

"Pardon me. Is that the place where the parking lot slopes downward to the south?" I asked.

"So I parked my car in the far corner, hundreds of

feet from every other car, and walked up to the market entrance."

I wanted to ask Stanley if he had parked down in the ravine near the poorly designed drainage swale, but he was becoming more upset by the moment. I let him do the talking.

"I couldn't have been gone five lousy minutes. When I came out, I could see this unattended shopping cart at the top of the lot, maybe 500 feet from my car. It was heading downhill. So I started to sprint toward my Jag, but I was still about 800 feet away -"

"Oh no!"

"Yes. It got there before I did," he proclaimed with a somberness generally reserved for funerals. "It put a quarter inch dent in the side panel. You can see all 12 layers of hand-rubbed paint."

"Oh no!"

"Yes. Here's the repair estimate."

Przylutsky had come prepared. He handed me a three page print-out from an autobody shop.

"$3,827.33!" I gasped. "Oh no!"

"Yes. It'll be in the shop a month," Stanley lamented. "I want to sue!"

I began to explain the costs associated with litigation as well as my legal fee.

"I can't afford that," he said flatly. "I've got to make car payments each month."

That evening I needed some milk, so I decided to visit the scene of the crime. I parked my Buick in the far corner of the lot. When I returned, a shopping cart was resting against my car. I couldn't discern where the point of impact was, but I did note a quarter inch dent in the front of the cart.

"God! I hope they don't sue me," I thought to myself.

CHAPTER TWENTY:
LOST IN THE RAIN FOREST

It is possible to work diligently on a project, expending countless hours of energy, and large sums of money, only to find that no one is actually interested in the end product. Frankenstein learned this sad truth after completion of his monster, and Henry Ford did, too, after Edsels began rolling off the assembly line. One thing is certain: It's easier to write a book than it is to sell it. I had this naïve dream: I wanted my writing published. So one day I summoned all my courage and reached for the phone. Having studied the *Guide to Literary Agents* from cover to cover, I was now properly prepared to retain an agent and take my place among other literary geniuses and Pulitzer prize winners.

The phone rang - somewhere in Manhattan. That's where all the big important agents did business. It was just a matter of time before I'd speak with the agent dedicated to the publication of my manuscript. Together we'd make literary history. My heart jumped with school-boy anticipation.

"Snippit Literary Agents. May I help you?"
"Hello. This is Larry Fox. I was wondering if - "
"Who?"
"Larry Fox."
"Who's your agent?"
"No, this is the first time I've - "
"You're not a client?"
"No, you see .... that's why I'm calling. I'd like to

publish my - "

"You're not a published author?"

"No, but I was hoping that - "

"I'm sorry. You'll have to call back once you're published." Click!

The next 27 inquiries played out much the same. The chicken. The egg. The agent. The writer. How did anyone ever get a manuscript published? I needed answers. I saw an ad for the local writers' support group. What did I have to lose?

I slipped into the next meeting and took a seat in the back. About 70 struggling unpublished authors sat hoping in quiet desperation, that his or her big break was just around the corner. Lucy Schmidgill was nearing completion of her treatise on *Halloween Customs During the Great Depression.* Amos Feldspar was still trying to peddle his romance entitled *Glowing Embers Among the Petunias.*

People talked, sympathized, listened. All in all, it was like an AA meeting. Once in a while a member would stand, offer an observation or tender a confession, perhaps about how the poor soul had almost given up hope and had thrown an entire tablet of unused writing paper in the garbage. After the gasps had subsided, everyone would call out the speaker's name in encouragement, to let the poor slob know that even though he was unpublished, he wasn't a failure. At least not in the group's eyes. Some guy in the first row stood up.

"I'm Herbie."

"Hi, Herbie," everyone called out in unison.

"Hi, Herbie," I sang out in a solo voice, a split second after everyone else. Everyone turned and stared at me. Now I was unpublished *and* embarrassed.

"Agents," he lamented. "They won't talk to you unless you're published, and you can't get published without one. What's a guy like me to do?"

Everyone shook his head in support-group unison. So did I, a split second later. This guy knew his writing had merit. He just needed a forum in which the public could observe his genius. I felt his pain. Another lost soul rose to the occasion.

"I'm Bertram."

"Hi, Bertram," everyone shouted.

"Believe it or not," Bertram said, "agents are a dying breed. You don't need one. Not today. You can self-publish on your lap-top, and sell your manuscript world-wide on the Internet."

The unpublished dropped its collective jaw, then soon broke out in a round of applause. Bertram had the floor.

"Listen, agents are but one way to skin a cat. The other way is rainforest.com. I'm telling you. Get yourselves up off all fours. Stop begging and start self-publishing. We, my friends, can join the hottest trend in literature."

"Rainforest.com. What is that?" I muttered to myself. The aspiring author sitting to my right overheard me.

"You sell your book on the web. That way you skip the cost and hassle of an agent. You go directly to the reader."

"Wow. Thanks," I replied. "That's great info. This is my first time here."

"Well, don't just sit there. Let everyone know," my new friend Gilbert urged. I looked around the room. These were kindred spirits. I shed my inhibitions.

"Hi, I'm Larry," I shouted as I stood up.

"Hi, Larry," everyone shouted back.

This was just the beginning. Armed with a renewed confidence gained at the monthly support group meetings, I began to save my money, and in three short months I had enough to self-publish a thousand copies of my book. I was ready to enter the Rain Forest.

I love computers and the Internet. They make life so simple. Soon after I began practicing law back in 1973, I bought my first electric typewriter. I no longer had to press so hard on the keys. They hit the paper as if by magic. This new found efficiency increased my output at the office by 10 percent. I could produce as much as 12 pages of typed material a day. Twenty-five years later, computers run my law office, and my life. My daily output of printed material has become limitless. A 400-page contract can be scanned into my computer, re-edited, spell-checked, printed, and faxed to any country in the world in under 30 minutes.

Funny though, back when I was hand-typing legal documents, I drove a new car that ran on gas costing 30 cents a gallon. A mere $3 and the tank was full. I was good to go. What's more, the attendant gave out new drinking glasses or dinnerware. Today I can reproduce the contents of the Library of Congress with the touch of a button, but I'm driving a used car, and if I want to fill the tank, assuming gas is available, I need to refinance my house.

I hate computers and the Internet. They make life so complex. Years ago I could complete an entire title search at the courthouse without electricity. I'd lift one ancient deed book after another out of its spot, and read the original recorded document, just as generations of other attorneys before me had done. I loved touching the old leather-bound books. It was as if I were caressing a part of our county's history. Nowadays, a title search is done at a computer terminal if, indeed, the computer is "up" that day. If it's "down," it can set the title search - and me - back for days.

The truth is that I both love and hate computers and the Internet that controls us. Twenty-year-old Jake, our computer repairman, on the other hand, simply worships this new technology. He would rather install an updated computer program than take a walk in a rose garden after a summer rain. For Jake, life didn't actually begin until the advent of the Internet. If he needs to eat, he faxes an order to some fast food joint that delivers right to his door. If he wants to road-trip, he prints out a map with the most direct route reflecting the timing of each traffic light. Furniture or clothing? In the span of 10 minutes he can browse, select, order and pay. His newly purchased oversized pants are on his doorstep in less than 48 hours.

Jake rarely left his computer screen. It was his only

source of entertainment, sustenance, and employment. It was the means by which he communicated and interacted with other human beings.

I decided to call Jake to see if he could help me find my way into the Rain Forest. It was Saturday, and he was relaxing at home.

"Sure, come on over. Don't knock. Just come in. I'm downstairs."

Somehow I knew that.

Jake didn't like to answer his door personally. That took time away from the screen. Soon I found myself sitting side-by-side with Jake, staring into cyberspace. He had just e-mailed his grandmother in Tucson while ordering a pair of shoes for delivery on Monday.

"Larry, my man. What can I do for you?" Jake asked, his eyes never leaving the screen glowing 10 inches from his face. Jake wasn't being impolite. Rather, having only communicated with computers during his last 15 years, he had forgotten how to interact face-to-face.

"Jake," I began, "I recently self-published a book. Now, I'd like to sell it on the web."

I tried to sound like I knew what I was talking about.

"Nothing to it, Larry. You want to visit rainforest.com."

Funny - I hadn't seen Jake at the writer's support group meeting and yet he knew all about the Rain Forest. I watched in awe as his computer screen began to transform itself from a catalog displaying men's shoe sizes, into a book distribution franchise.

Welcome to the Rain Forest. So you're a writer! Here at Rain Forest, we make it easy for millions of readers worldwide to discover and buy your book.

I fell in love with the Rain Forest. It was the first time anyone or anything had expressed the slightest interest in my writing. I couldn't wait to get started. The directions from cyber headquarters were disarmingly simple. I was instructed to send two of my books to an address in Iowa. If the manuscript was found to be suitable for sale to the public, some book reviewer laboring deep within the Rain Forest would retain the two volumes on consignment, and try to sell them. I would receive 50 percent of the sale price.

That sounded fair enough. I sent two of my books by overnight mail to this unseen browser of the written word - someone with whom I had neither spoken nor met. Somebody who lived in a pretend rain forest in Iowa.

What if the books were returned as unsuitable? What if no one out of the "millions of readers worldwide" decided to buy my book? What if my writing was crap? One week later, I got an e-mail from Iowa.

Receipt of two books acknowledged.

Acknowledged by whom*?*

A week later, I received a second e-mail.

Two books sold. Your reference number for all future correspondence is 473827764793AP8-R. Your sales ratio is 3,457,729. You will receive payment for the above two sales by the first of the next month.

I remember when I was served notice from my draft board for the scheduling of a physical. I also recall when the certified letter arrived from the Pennsylvania Bar Examiners, the contents of which would announce whether or not I had passed the State Bar Examination. These two missives caused my heart to race for a day or two. But receipt of today's e-mail surpassed both.

In the twinkling of an eye, I joined the ranks of Hemingway, Poe, and Longfellow. Not only was I a published author, albeit self-published, now my work was being offered for sale and being purchased! By the first of next month I would receive a check for my labors. I could not contain my joy. Let's see - I sold two books at $15 each. I get 50 percent - glory be, I would soon receive a check for $15!

How foolish now appeared those Manhattan agents who turned me down cold. The joke was on them. Had one of them agreed to represent me, by the first of the next month, he'd have earned his 10 percent commission and would have been $1.50 richer for doing nothing. A golden opportunity squandered. Well, screw them. I was being published and purchased.

I studied my precious e-mail, but didn't quite understand the part about the sales ratio.

I e-mailed an inquiry and received a response the very next morning.

The Rain Forest maintains approximately four million book titles in stock. The 'sales ratio' figure denotes during the present fiscal year how well your book is selling in comparison to all other books in our inventory.

I did some quick calculations. Similar to a five-year-old, I used my fingers.

	4,000,000	Total books held in inventory
	-3,457,729	My sales ratio
=	542,271	Number of titles that have sold fewer copies than my book

If my arithmetic computations were correct, there were 542,271 different books held in inventory that had sold fewer than two copies during the last fiscal year. By comparison, my book was rapidly becoming an overnight success.

Within a week, I received another e-mail from the Rain Forest. They were ordering another six books. My new sales ratio number was 2,844,917. Apparently, with the exception of a lousy 2,844,917 other books, I was their top seller! I love the Internet.

Two weeks later, there was yet another e-mail from the Rain Forest. They wanted another eight books. I fired them off by overnight mail. My new sales ratio figure had fallen to 1,080,498. I had sold a total of 16 books circulating world-wide in less than a month. I had only 984 volumes left from my initial printing of 1,000. As I surveyed the cartons of books stacked in my living room, I pondered the feasibility of a second printing.

Then came the invitation from the writer's support group. Now that I was an internationally recognized author, they wanted me as a guest speaker. The letter closed with the observation: "You are an inspiration to us all."

I have been telling short stories to my friends for years. At the conclusion of each anecdote comes a reaction from the listener - sometimes good - sometimes not so good. But favorable or not, to a writer any response is reward in itself. Only after my book began to sell did I begin to realize that people I shall never meet are reading my thoughts at locations and times, both of which are unknown to me. I won't be there to soak in the luxury of their various reactions.

Once in a while I have this dream. I am walking on a deserted beach, the surf and ocean spray spreading their magic elixir into the atmosphere. Seabirds call to me as I meander barefoot among the dissipating waves. And then I see her. A woman sitting alone in a beach chair. She is reading a book. As I approach, I realize it's my book. She doesn't notice me. She begins to laugh out loud. Again and again. At that point, serene contentment envelopes me, and I realize that I will die a happy man.

CHAPTER TWENTY-ONE:
THE HALLOWEEN DECORATION

The changing temperatures and crisp winds announced the arrival of October, a time for falling leaves and my favorite holiday: Halloween. Little goblins always venture to my door, screaming "Trick or Treat!" I usually act scared, then hand out the good stuff - Butterfingers, Hershey Bars and Snickers. Those were *my* favorites when I journeyed door-to-door in what seems like 100 years ago. Now the folks who gave me candy have all passed on, to take their place as ghosts.

I turned to my law office secretary.

"Cathy," I reminisced, "let's do it up this year. I'm talking spooky city. It'll be great. We'll scare the clients to death, this time, before they get our bill!"

"O.K. I'll see what I can find," she agreed.

Coincidentally, October is also budgetary hearings month at the courthouse. County Council convenes each fall to determine how monies should be allocated among the various local governmental offices, all of which seek tax revenues to provide their services. As legal counsel for the coroner, I have often been called upon to assist in the preparation and presentation of his proposed annual budgets.

"It's the same damn thing every year, Fox," Mortimer Grey lamented in the privacy of his third floor courthouse office. "Demands on my department increase as my budget goes down the toilet."

I was, as usual, having difficulty focusing on the coroner. A life-size color-coded replica of a human body situated behind him had once again stolen my attention. This macabre figure exposed every organ, muscle and tissue. It was entitled "The Post Mortem Anatomical Relief." It was poorly named, for I didn't derive any relief from it at all. Dangling next to this dissected body was a full-scale model of a human skeleton, composed of interconnected ivory-white plastic bones. These two displays gave me the creeps.

"Now that's what we need at the office this year," I mused to myself as Mortimer rattled on about financial constraints. Realistically speaking, though, he wasn't just blowing smoke. My initial review of county council's proposed budgetary cuts confirmed that almost every requested line item had been drastically decreased.

"I can't work like this," he protested. "Of all things, I'm short on supplies. Things that might come in handy here. Like, oh, I don't know ... body bags? What am I supposed to use when I run out? Saran Wrap?"

Grey's private emergency line rang. "Pardon me," he apologized as he reached for the phone.

"Uh huh ... When? ... Yes ... Which side of the river? ... Yes ... Right ... I'll send Bob over when he gets back. Don't touch a thing until he gets there."

In minutes, he had his assistant on the phone.

"Bob ... Get down to Tressel Bridge at 8th. Cops found a body. No, I've got budgetary hearings with Larry the rest of the day. Thanks."

This was, indeed, a busy office. Just yesterday, two hunters had stumbled upon an intact human skull. Today's newspaper reported that the remains might belong to none other than Lapaige Lipshitz, a notorious local mobster who had been missing for more than a year. Lipshitz had a significant underbite, similar to a crocodile. The skull apparently did, too. A check of dental records would confirm the identity.

Having put out that fire, Grey began to refocus upon his budgetary problems.

"Where were we?" he asked.

"Uh ... Saran Wrap?"

"Huh? Oh, yeah. Body bags. I'm low on everything. We've even started using store-bought containers for some of the smaller body parts we find. It's so unprofessional."

I genuinely enjoyed the coroner's company. He wasn't the usual pontificating bureaucrat who continually sought to justify his existence. Grey was a truly dedicated public servant who pinched every penny. As a former third-generation steel worker, he had never even abandoned his cost-conscious habit of carrying his homemade bagged lunch to the office. He always placed it out of the way on the window sill overlooking the parking deck.

We studied the mound of accounting documents that served as the basis for our budgetary requests. Our public hearing with the finance subcommittee was scheduled to commence at 11:30 a.m. sharp, in a mere half hour. Grey gave his secretary some last minute instructions, and then we gathered our papers and walked upstairs to the public hearing room. It was clear we'd have neither the time nor luxury to have lunch before our appearance at council chambers. I left my lunch bag behind with his.

The seven council members had campaigned vigorously during last year's county-wide election, each pledging not to raise taxes. The coroner's proposed budget seeking a 150% increase in operating funds was not well-received, despite Grey's forceful argument.

For two hours, we fielded questions posed by council members. They promised to give our requests "due consideration." We were back in Grey's office by 2:00 p.m. Then he got an emergency call from the hospital. He quickly thanked me and left. I remembered I had a meeting back in Bethlehem, so I grabbed my files and lunch, and headed for the car.

During the next week, Cathy did a whiz-bang job decorating the office. There were ghoulish goblins in the first floor windows, and dancing spooks in the waiting room. An artificial amputated plastic arm and matching mutilated leg greeted clients in the vestibule. But the decoration that had everyone talking was the skull suspended outside the front door. Cathy had installed two small white lights in the eye sockets. It added an eerie glow to the old noggin.

"You sure did pull out all the stops this year," I boasted to Cathy as we sat together in the library having lunch. Similar to the coroner, we rarely ever ventured out or ordered in. I brought a tuna fish salad bagel, my favorite. Cathy munched on her usual egg salad sandwich.

"Part of the credit goes to you, Larry," Cathy suggested. "Where on earth did you find such a life-like skull? The jaw looks so real, and some of the teeth with the silver fillings could pass for the actual thing!"

"What do you mean? I didn't have time to shop for Halloween," I confessed between bites. "What skull are you talking about?"

Cathy smiled. "Hello? The one you left in the bag on your desk. I hung it up as soon as I found it. The lights for the eye sockets came from the dollar store."

"I didn't leave any skull on my desk," I protested.

We both stopped chewing, and stared confusedly at one another. That's when the phone rang.

"This has never happened before," Mortimer explained in a panic. "I've lost a skull. The DA's all over me. Says it's Lapaige Lipshitz's head. Of course, I was out of bags again, so last week I stored it in a brown bag near my window. Yesterday, when I reached for it, all I found was some old foul-smelling tuna sandwich."

"Mort - can I call you back in five minutes?"

"Is there a problem?"

"Five minutes, Mort."

I hung up, and slowly walked toward the front door. I studied the blinking eye sockets of the former mobster, now reincarnated as Halloween art. I hated to take him down. Where would I find another skull half as scary?

CHAPTER TWENTY-TWO:
THE DISALLOWED DEDUCTION

George Orloski worked 72 hours a week. He didn't have much choice. As the sole owner of Orloski's Overalls, he monitored every facet of his small struggling business. It had always been a marginal enterprise - under-funded and burdened by debt that never seemed to subside. When George started the business 30 years ago in his garage, he took out a $70,000 personal loan, using his twin home as collateral. Now he had 12 employees and six delivery trucks and carried a $300,000 bank loan and a $50,000 line of credit with a balance almost always near its maximum. Each April 15th was more unnerving than the last. He even thought about selling one of his trucks to cover tax debt.

Worry had made him old. He was 59, but he looked 79. And he was trapped - too old to find another job, and too far in debt to sell his business at a profit. Who would want it anyway? If there were an annual profit at all, it was marginal. Each of his truck drivers made more than he did. He was lucky to clear $25,000 a year.

This business was not composed of the exciting stuff from which movie scripts are born. George cleaned industrial overalls and work uniforms for local industries. The heater repairman who serviced my oil furnace showed up at my house wearing one of George's outfits. He left an hour later, a sooty mess. It was one of George's industrial strength laundry machines that removed the stains and assured delivery of fresh clean uniforms by the next work week.

Still, George was an imaginative entrepreneur. Two years earlier, he decided to expand his horizons: He entered the diaper cleaning business after other companies had abandoned the service.

"Not everyone wants to use disposables," he explained. "A lot of parents these days see the environmental benefits of cloth."

George went deeper into debt. He bought another washing machine the size of a dump truck, and took a chance and purchased 10,000 cloth diapers. If his weekend helpers called in sick, George dragged himself to work on Sundays to operate the gigantic apparatus himself.

I was George's lawyer, and his friend. I had known him since his steel plant days. He started the overall cleaning business after he was laid off. I knew him when his first wife died 20 years ago, leaving him with four kids to raise. He put each one through college. I attended his wedding 10 years ago, when he married for the second time. Now he and his new wife Diana had a 9-year-old daughter. Except for the wedding, I can't recall having ever spent any time with his wife. I only saw George at my office or at his cleaning business. Diana was usually at home caring for their daughter.

It was 6:00 p.m. and George was banging on my office door. He didn't have an appointment. He looked like death.

"I came home at five, after working 12 hours, and all her stuff was gone. So is my daughter. Here's the note."

He handed me a crumpled piece of paper.

Dear George:
I can't stand you any more. You are the most
boring person I have ever met. All you
think about is overalls and diapers. There's
more to life than cleaning industrial uniforms.
I've finally met someone with a zest for life,
the vacuum cleaner salesman. Good-bye.
Diana

There are two types of divorces: those you see coming, and those you don't.

"How was I supposed to know she was unhappy? She never said a thing." A tear fell on his industrial overalls.

"Did you two ever talk?" I asked.

"Yes. Maybe. No. I don't know. I was working around the clock trying to keep a roof over our heads. There wasn't a whole lot of time for casual chit-chat. I usually came home and collapsed in bed."

Diana retained Olivia Callus, Esquire. She specialized in protecting defenseless females. She filed for spousal and child support. George asked me to represent him. I contacted Callus to see if she objected to my entry of appearance on behalf of George.

"Have you ever represented Mrs. Orloski?" she asked.

"No, just Mr. Orloski and his cleaning business," I confirmed.

"O.K. Be my guest," she replied. "I'll see you in court."

One week later, I received notice of the scheduling of a domestic relations conference in three months. More than 400 other domestic relations cases languished ahead of ours.

"Should I pay her support now, or wait until the proceeding?" George inquired.

"Pay her each week, starting immediately," I advised. "Otherwise, you'll incur a delinquency, since the support obligation commences when the original petition was filed."

"Even if she left for no reason?"

"Even if you were a good and faithful husband."

George stared at me with a look in his eye that suggested the law didn't make much sense.

"What do I owe?"

"It all depends on how much you make. Support for a wife and child is based upon a percentage of your income, along with several other factors, such as her income, medical expenses, and other legitimate deductions."

"She doesn't work outside the home."

"What did you earn during the last six months?"

"I make $25,000 a year."

I reviewed the support charts while George sat silently, thinking, gazing at me, his financial fate resting within the circuitry of my calculator.

"You'll have to pay about 40% of your net income each week."

George did some quick computations in his head.

"But that's over $200 a week. I can't afford that!"

"I'm sorry," I responded in the sympathetic tone I always use during support consultations. "The law is written to protect mothers and children."

"But I didn't do anything wrong," George offered in a confused and distant manner. "Nothing ... " he repeated as he reached for his keys and left my office.

George faithfully carried out my advice. Each week he sent his wife $220. As a result, his commercial loan payments fell behind, and became delinquent. He decided to diminish his salary so his company would have sufficient funds to make the payments. Each night he returned to a dark, lonely house. After 12 hours of backbreaking work, he fell into a fitful sleep.

On the eve of George's long awaited support conference, I called to confirm our 10:00 o'clock appointment scheduled more than three months ago.

We met outside the domestic relations office 15 minutes early.

"Would you believe those guards upstairs confiscated my nail clipper?" he complained. "Great catch on their part. Did they really think I'd jump someone and give them a manicure?"

We entered the newly installed waiting room, a 20' x 30' closet in which couples, who hated one another, got to sit practically on top of each other while waiting for their cases to be called. A seasoned uniformed sheriff's deputy stood at the ready, with gun, baton, mace, two-way radio, and badge.

A receptionist sat on the other side of a two-inch thick bullet-proof window, safely separated from deadly nail clippers and shifty attorneys.

She might have been 25, probably had never exercised a day in her life, and was dining on a chocolate bar. She worked the phones and refused to acknowledge my presence even as I stood two feet before her. She was already irritated, despite the early morning hour. Finally, she reluctantly opened the partition a quarter inch.

"Which hearing?" she barked, rolling her eyes upward.

"Orloski," I said clearly and carefully, recognizing my window of opportunity was open, however narrowly.

"Are all counsel and parties present?"

"The plaintiff and her attorney aren't here yet."

She glared at me as if I had just slapped her.

"Then sit down and come back when *all* members of your party are present," she admonished, as she slammed the window shut.

Where the hell was Attorney Callus and her client? *They* had requested this hearing - not me. The sheriff, my client, and an unhappy couple, comprised the other occupants of this stuffy dungeon. I made the fatal mistake of taking the remaining seat between Romeo and Juliet. He was about 30, and was battling the lingering effects of a hangover. She was in her late 20s and was wearing dark Jackie Kennedy sunglasses.

"Bitch," the first shot rang out from my left.

"Prick," came the return fire from the right.

"You had to clean me out, didn't you."

"You had to nail your secretary, didn't you."

"Say," I piped up with a smile. "Would you two like to sit together?"

"And by the way, where's the air conditioner? Did you take that too?"

Mercifully, Attorney Callus finally appeared at the doorway, her client in tow. She sauntered confidently over to the plate glass window and tapped on it with her French manicured fingernails. The receptionist perked up, smiled, waved hello, and pressed a secret buzzer. Just like that, the door to the inner sanctum swung open.

Callus lead our entourage to the hearing room at the end of the hall. Workers carried files into a variety of offices along the corridor, while still others labored intently to remove those same files and take them elsewhere.

Callus strode into the windowless hearing room. It was so small we'd have to take turns breathing. We sat at a miniature table across from each other. All of our feet touched. The hearing officer, Ms. Featherstone, sat at her own petite desk, similar to one I had used in kindergarten.

"Orloski?" she inquired.

"Orloski," Callus affirmed.

Featherstone neither looked up nor acknowledged anyone.

"Mr. Orloski - your social security number?"

He responded.

"Your address?

"Place of employment?

"Number of children?

"Date of marriage?

"Birth date?

"Any tattoos or visible scars?

"Date of separation?"

Featherstone pivoted to her left, but this time looked up and forced a smile. She asked the same questions of Mrs. Orloski, with one exception. Apparently if she possessed any tattoos or visible scars, it didn't matter. Something was in the air, but I wasn't sure what.

At one time Featherstone might have been considered handsome, almost pretty. But she had labored too long in the windowless bowels of the domestic relations office. It had robbed her of her soul and any spontaneous humor or kindness. I had seen corpses with more personality.

"Mr. Orloski, do you agree that you owe child support?"

"Yes. Brittany is my child."

"Do you agree to pay spousal support?"

"No, that's where I draw the line. She left me for no

reason. She cheated on me. If her new man is so wonderful, then he should support her, or she should get her own job."

"So noted," Ms. Featherstone mumbled.

"Now, did you bring your last three tax returns?"

"Yes."

My client reached into a paper bag and produced the requested forms. Ms. Featherstone stuck her hand out again without looking up. Then she studied the tax returns for what seemed an eternity. I could taste Callus' cheap artificial rose perfume, or was it Mrs. Orloski's? It made me sick to my stomach. The room swirled. Was this claustrophobic closet becoming smaller?

Ms. Featherstone ended her extensive perusal of my client's tax returns.

"You've reported income of $25,000 annually during each of the last three years," she observed again without lifting her head, or making eye contact.

"Yes," Mr. Orloski acknowledged the obvious. "My family and I have lived simply. My company doesn't generate much of a profit."

"But I note here that you have, during each of the three years, purchased over $150,000 worth of new overalls, uniforms, and most recently diapers."

"Yes," my client confirmed. "As the old inventory becomes torn, too soiled, or otherwise unusable, it must be replaced."

"Do you have any documented proof that such an extensive replacement of inventory was warranted?" Ms. Featherstone demanded.

Mr. Orloski stopped short. He was as confused as I was. "Proof?" he repeated. "What do you mean 'proof'? I look at each stinkin' diaper and each uniform when it comes back. If it's beyond repair or below the standards my clientele expects, I discard it and buy a new one. If I didn't restock my inventory as necessary, my clients would bail."

"But the discarding of inventory, which results in the costly repurchase of new product ... that appears to be a subjective evaluation made solely by you. Correct?"

"Yes. That's what I do. It's called running a business," Orloski confirmed.

"Yet you have no documentation to reflect the reasoning why a certain item of clothing might be discarded or retained."

"Of course not. I've been tossing defective goods for over 30 years. I don't discard usable product. How cost-effective would that be?"

"That's not for me to judge," Featherstone countered, her head still buried in the file.

I had to step in. "Um ... Ms. Featherstone?"

"What?" she snapped, finally looking up.

"My client can easily secure the testimony of his accountant to certify that the purchase of new inventory is a necessity," I suggested.

"We don't permit third party witnesses. The domestic relations office doesn't conduct trials. We hear from the parties, themselves. That's it. Otherwise, we'd be here all day."

"Ms. Featherstone?" I interjected again.

"Now what?"

"The IRS has never questioned the $150,000 annual purchase of new inventory as a legitimate business expense. Neither my client nor his company has ever been audited. The federal government accepts my client's annual income as reported - $25,000. Mrs. Orloski, who also signed the tax forms, has lived on that income for years."

"I'm not the IRS, counselor, and its rules don't apply to domestic relations orders. My job is to insure that children and spouses in need receive adequate support. From where I sit, it appears that your client could have made six figures this year, but chose to stock up on diapers instead. His unfortunate business decision will not dissuade the domestic relations office from performing its duty."

My further protestations didn't appear to sway the fiscally conservative Featherstone. Diaper depreciation was an accounting concept unknown to her.

"Will there be anything else?" she asked at the

conclusion of my useless suggestions.

I looked in disbelief at George, and he back at me.

"Very well. I'll issue a proposed support order by next week. Upon receipt of same, should either party dispute my findings, you will have 10 days in which to file an appeal before the Court of Common Pleas."

"That was a one-way ass-kicking, wasn't it?" George astutely observed as we left the hearing room and walked down the hallway. We stopped to permit a clerk carrying files to enter a room on the left. Another office worker emerged from the same room, carrying files destined for a room on the right.

We stopped out in the hallway to discuss the potential impact of today's hearing.

"I feel Featherstone will only give you a partial deduction for new inventory you had to purchase. That'll increase the amount of support you'll have to pay," I cautioned.

"Great," George noted. "Diana knows I've never made a dime over $25,000."

So did Uncle Sam, the Commonwealth of Pennsylvania, and the City of Bethlehem, all of which imposed and collected various taxes based on income.

Ms. Featherstone, on the other hand, was not quite so gullible. She could see right through George's little scheme to avoid paying support, and this was one time the domestic relations office would assure that justice prevailed.

- - - - - - - - - - - - -

I didn't think I would see George quite so soon, but there he was, standing at my office door, a letter clutched in his hand. Featherstone had chosen to disallow *any* deduction for the purchase of replacement inventory. As a result, she had determined that George, as sole owner of his company, earned $175,000 per year, composed of $25,000 in salary and $150,000 in income he could have taken if only he hadn't attempted to conceal it with unnecessary purchases of diapers and overalls.

"You are to be commended, George. According to this, you earned $175,000 this year," I noted, sarcasm rolling off my tongue.

"Yeah. I saw that. I'm freakin' rich and never knew it."

"Says so right here," I confirmed.

The second page displayed further computations based upon George's corrected adjusted gross income, as determined by Ms. Featherstone. She directed that he pay child and spousal support of $4,800 per month.

"I only make $25,000 a year," he reminded me.

The third page continued to paint a disquieting picture.

"That's the part that talks about arrearages," he instructed me.

Featherstone had determined that because George had only paid $220 a week during the three month period prior to the conference, he now maintained a delinquency of $11,800, that continued to increase at the rate of $160 per day.

"I can't afford that," George advised me.

"I'll take an appeal," I promised him.

- - - - - - - - - - - - -

I didn't think I would see George quite so soon, but there he was, standing at my office door. It had only been a week since we reviewed Ms. Featherstone's computations, prompting me to file an appeal with the Court of Common Pleas.

"My trucks are gone. They took the company checking account, too."

"What trucks?"

"My three delivery vans. Now I can't deliver diapers, and I can't disburse payroll. They said they'd deduct what they get for the vans from the arrearages I owe."

Had Featherstone not received my notice of appeal?

Didn't the appeal suspend further action by her office, pending review by the court? A conference was in order. I called the domestic relations office.

"All associates are unavailable," voicemail announced. "Please be advised that the domestic relations office does not accept telephonic inquires. Please schedule an appointment. Your call is being monitored for quality assurance ... Buenos Dias. El officio domestico ... "

I slammed down the phone. Now I knew why a two-inch bullet-proof partition separated domestic relations from the rest of the world.

Every passing hour brought financial disaster closer to George's door. There was only one thing to do while waiting for the court to hear his appeal. A letter to Attorney Callus. She was a tough advocate, but she wasn't nuts like Featherstone.

Dear Attorney Callus:

An appeal in the above matter has been filed, and will be heard by the court in approximately two months. By the time this matter is reviewed, my client will amass an artificial arrearage of almost $19,000, even if he continues to pay $220 per week in support. I believe the court will ultimately determine that Mr. Orloski only earns $25,000 per year and that the arrearage should be voided. Unfortunately, the sheriff has already taken possession of my client's commercial vehicles and has garnished the company checking account. As a result, his business cannot operate, and nine employees are about to lose their jobs. Would you please ask your client to agree to accept $220 per week until the appeal is heard, and will you further confirm that the sheriff may return the company vehicles so that my client can continue to generate

income and ultimately pay support. Thank you
for your consideration of this request.

> *Very truly yours,*
> *Larry Fox*

Time was of the essence, so I faxed the letter immediately. Soon Attorney Callus was on the phone.

"Hello. Just got your fax, Fox."

"Thank you for responding so quickly."

"Not a problem. But look, I'm not going to ... say, have you ever heard about the 75-year-old man who was sentenced to 30 years for armed robbery?"

"No, can't say that I have."

"He told the judge he couldn't possibly serve all that time - that he'd probably die first. Know what the judge said?"

"No."

"Do as much time as you can. Fox, that's my advice to your client."

"Does that mean you won't agree to the return of his company vehicles?"

"Listen, I have a support order for $4,800 per month in my back pocket. You want me to commit legal malpractice and tear it up? I'm supposed to be an aggressive advocate for my client - not a bleeding heart. If your client doesn't have the money, tell him to sell some of his diapers. See you in court, Fox." Click.

- - - - - - - - - -

I didn't think I would see George so soon, but there he was standing at my office door for the third time. After all, it was just yesterday Callus and I spoke. George didn't look well.

"The sheriff just took my car - the old Pontiac. It's going to be sold, too, to decrease the amount of my arrearages. That isn't the half of it," he continued. "Another letter."

I read the formal document in silence. His bank had received notice to lock his safe deposit box and freeze his personal checking and savings accounts.

The sheriff sale of the three business vans, the Pontiac, and liquidation of the bank accounts and safe deposit box fetched a princely sum of just $13,547. In just two short weeks, the court would hear George's appeal. Unfortunately, arrearages now totaled $18,100. George was short $4,553, and the deficiency continued to grow at the rate of $160 a day. So the sheriff picked up George for non-support, and threw him in jail. George didn't seem to mind. He had run out of food at home anyway, and the power had been turned off. He called collect from the county prison.

"Is my appeal still scheduled for next week?"

"Yes, it is," I assured him.

"Good. See you then."

They brought George over in leg irons and handcuffs. Arrearages had now built up to about $6,000.

"That's a boatload of money," Judge Pearson observed over his wire-rimmed bifocals. "Did you apply for work release while you were in confinement?"

"No," George responded. "Thanks to all this, my company went belly-up. There is no job to go to."

His Honor looked confused. "It says here you are the president and sole owner of a business and that you make an adjusted net income of $175,000 a year." The judge continued to shuffle through a stack of papers prepared by the domestic relations office.

"I only make $25,000 a year, Judge. That's what my wife and I have reported to the IRS during the last three years, and that's what we've lived on."

The judge stared at the quartet standing before him. Mrs. Orloski, Attorney Callus, George and me.

"Take those ridiculous shackles off of him," he ordered the sheriff. "Now what the hell is going on here?"

And so I told him, about Ms. Featherstone, the diapers, and the disallowed deduction for new inventory.

His Honor stared ahead in disbelief.

"Anyone who knows anything realizes you can't get more than five or six poops out of a cloth diaper before it's time to replace it," Judge Pearson noted.

"No more than four if prunes are involved, sir," the bailiff chimed in from behind.

"I'll take judicial notice of that," the judge continued. "Even strained carrots can leave an unworkable stain. Featherstone should have acknowledged that fact, and allowed the deduction for new inventory. I'm telling you, it's unimaginable what happens when some little bundle of joy consumes a jar of fruit. I remember back to the first time I served apricots to my daughter. She was just three months old, but that didn't stop her from taking a - "

"Your Honor?"

"Yes, Attorney Fox?"

"Allowance of the diaper depreciation deduction diminishes my client's adjusted net income to $25,000. As a result, the support chart only requires a weekly payment of $220. The sheriff sold my client's car, three vans, and liquidated bank assets, generating monies totaling $13,547. This sum was paid to Mrs. Orloski despite the fact she received $220 each week."

"Then Mr. Orloski has a $13,547 credit," the court declared. "By my calculations, he probably won't have to pay support for the next one to two years. Case dismissed. You are released from custody, Mr. Orloski."

I drove George back home. Because he no longer had to pay support, he soon qualified for a small bank loan. He bought back the company vans, and started washing diapers and overalls again.

Ms. Featherstone, conversely, was ordered by the court to enroll in Accounting 101 at the local community college. She refused, choosing instead to take early retirement. She was last seen in a local nursing home, wearing a diaper.

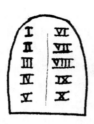

CHAPTER TWENTY-THREE:
THE OATH

The truly great architect has, through the ages, sought to accomplish more than the mere design of a building or monument. He or she has realized that an extraordinary structure can, by its very presence, profoundly affect those who dwell or labor within its confines.

The architect who designed Courtroom No. 1 at the Northampton County Courthouse, located in Easton, Pennsylvania, was such a visionary. Whenever I am privileged to enter this Civil War Era temple of justice, I am immediately transformed from a mere mortal, into a sworn defender of the downtrodden, and advocate for the unjustly accused. In my mind, I present a hundred persuasive arguments, even though neither jury nor judge is present. It's this courtroom that generates the metamorphosis. Those stuffy courtrooms in the newly constructed Federal Courthouse in Allentown, the courtrooms desecrated by fluorescent lighting and windows that don't open, were probably designed by someone burdened by both a limited governmental budget, and no imagination or love for the law. Such rooms could just as easily serve as the location for an insurance company office, or a shoe repair drop-off.

Last week I stole a few moments to sit alone among the rows of 80-foot hand-hewn walnut pews that have patiently reposed within Courtroom No. 1 for more than a century and a half. These polished wooden benches have, since our first encounter, been my silent friends, for they and I share such intimate and cherished memories. They once stood as witnesses to my admission to the Northampton County Bar. I was so very young, and didn't even know it. My mother and father sat over there, in the third row, proudly watching as I took the oath of attorney. They've been dead now for many years.

The pews were there to help celebrate when I won my first trial. After the jury returned with an acquittal, I sat over there with Mr. Musingo, the stenographer, and we laughed out loud for half an hour as we relived the bizarre testimony, and the unexpected verdict. Musingo was the last stenographer in the county to use pen and inkwell, transcribing each word by hand. He possessed neither computer nor apparatus powered by electrical current, yet he never missed a word. His simple tools were similar to those employed by the drafters of the Constitution, who likewise didn't miss a single precious phrase. Musingo has also disappeared from this hallowed courtroom, never to return, and I miss his gentle smile.

The pews have acted as silent onlookers as thousands of trials have passed into history. Both the great and the meek have taken refuge here, resting their weary, or nervous, or pompous bodies within the confines of the curved backs and comfortable wooden seats.

As I sit and ponder in the stillness, the portraits of generations of judges stare at me. It's such a privilege to practice law - to engage in civilized discourse before a neutral party, thereby avoiding physical confrontation. It has been a blessing from God to have made, at times, my living in this ornate chamber. And God is here in this temple dedicated to the law. For there can be no law unless a common thread is woven into the fabric of each individual who enters this sacred hall - a belief in a higher being.

It is ironic that it is the law of our land that guarantees the separation of Church and State, and yet the law cannot exist without acknowledgment of a higher authority - for those who enter this courtroom swear before the Almighty that they shall tell the truth. To dishonor the sworn oath by the uttering of a falsehood desecrates both the law, and this holy place.

My eye falls upon the massive bronze plaque that adorns the front wall of the courtroom to the left of the judges' seats. The plaque, which has, for more than a century, faced each spectator who has sat in the pews, quotes the Ten Commandments. These words stand as yet another irony, for if they were honored, there would be no need for any other laws, or for any lawyers.

There are those who have dared to defile this courtroom by use of false statements, in defiance of their sacred oath. They fail to understand that such indiscretion does not go unnoticed or unpunished. I recall, as do these pews, the case of Manuel Rosa Bandias.

It has been almost 25 years since that trial, but I remember it as if it were yesterday. It all began when seven Hispanic males entered Russo's Beverage Store on Bethlehem's South Monroe Street at about 8:50 p.m. Mrs. Geraldine Russo, a 70-year-old grandmother, and one of her grandsons, Matthew, were preparing to close up for the night. The rest of the family was attending a high school football game.

The seven conspirators quickly made their intentions known. One thug stood guard at the door, while others overpowered Matthew, who was bound, gagged, and thrown into a walk-in cooler. Another pushed Mrs. Russo aside and began to break open the cash register. Disappointed at the small amount of cash uncovered, another gangster approached the trembling Mrs. Russo, stuck a sawed-off shotgun in her face, and advised her in broken English that if she didn't tell him where the rest of the money was, he'd kill her and her grandson.

"My son already took the day's proceeds to the bank night depository, just before he went to the football game," Mrs. Russo sobbed hysterically.

The apparent ringleader of the group took charge. He sauntered up to within three inches of his victim's face, while the desperado who had brandished the shotgun held the elderly lady's hands behind her.

"You got hidden safe!"

"No!" she stammered.   "There is no other money here. I swear before Almighty God!"

The ringleader chose to disbelieve her.   He realized that Mrs. Russo was about to faint, and time was growing short.   He exposed a .38 caliber revolver he had hidden under his shirt.   He placed the weapon in his right hand, as he grabbed his hostage by the throat with his left hand.

"I no ask again!   Where all de other money?"

"There isn't any more.   I'd give it to you.   I swear!"

This response was unacceptable.   The cowardly felon, facing a woman three times his age, her hands restrained behind her, took a step backward in order to generate greater energy upon impact.   Repositioning the gun in his hand, he uncovered the plastic handle that he then raised, violently striking the grandmother in the face several times with the butt of the gun.   She collapsed in a pool of blood.   The desperados escaped with $76.45.

When Mrs. Russo and Matthew failed to return home, several family members headed straight for the beverage store to investigate.   They found Mrs. Russo near death, and Matthew suffering from hypothermia.   Mrs. Russo was rushed to the hospital.   Six teeth had been knocked out of her mouth, and her jaw was broken in two places.   One eye socket had been crushed, and unfortunately her eye could not be saved.   As a result of her injuries, the once self-sufficient lady was permanently institutionalized.

The robbers were now $76.45 wealthier from the evening's adventure.   They decided to celebrate their good fortune by patronizing the El Paso Cantina on East Third Street.   As the seven misfits drank, however, dissension in the ranks began to boil to the surface.   The cheap whiskey and watery beer only served to inflame their animated exchange.   The stolen loot would soon be expended, and it was now becoming apparent even to these inebriated fools that there might not be enough money left to buy the gas needed to return home to distant Brooklyn, New York, more than 80 miles and several tollbooths from Bethlehem.

As their voices rose in anger, it became easier for the bartender, who spoke Spanish, to overhear the dialogue of these strangers, who sauntered from the far corner of the beer-stained room out the door, pointing fingers and placing blame.

The outlaws didn't get very far. The bartender gave the police a description of the old Chevy they were driving, and suggested the desperados might stop at an all-night gas station as they proceeded east toward New York. The police spotted the car as it pulled into the mini-mart on City Line Avenue. The vehicle was quickly surrounded, and not a shot was fired. Arrested on charges of armed robbery, assault with intent to commit grievous bodily harm, carrying concealed deadly weapons, conspiracy, and auto theft, were Packo, Ringleader, Lookout, Shotgun, Angel, and Guzman. Guzman slept drunk through his 1:00 a.m. arraignment. The others growled intermittently at the magistrate, who had been awakened by the police to come to City Hall. This displeased His Honor, who decided to set bail for each defendant at $1 million. They were escorted to the Northampton County Prison, and placed in isolation cells until the results of involuntarily administered tuberculosis tests could be evaluated.

Detective Fonzone drove over to the El Paso Cantina the next afternoon to interview the bartender, Frank, personally and to thank him for his assistance. Frank confirmed what the victim Matthew, had also recalled from his hospital bed: There were seven criminals, not six.

"There were only six in the Chevy," the detective repeated.

"Seven in my Cantina last night," Frank affirmed.

The seventh thug, "Manuel," had made good on his earlier promise to find his way back to Brooklyn alone. After leaving the Cantina, he refrained from using any roadways, choosing rather to walk along railroad tracks that proceeded in an easterly direction. He progressed about 25 miles through the evening, and by daybreak, had crossed over the Delaware River trestle into New Jersey. When he tried to break into a vending machine outside Phillipsburg, an off-duty state trooper spotted him, and after a short footrace, tackled him to the ground.

The New Jersey authorities were aware of the brutal robbery in Pennsylvania and, believing that Manuel fit the description of the missing seventh conspirator, notified the Bethlehem Police of Manuel's arrest. Two weeks later, he was extradited from New Jersey, and charged with the same five felonies as his companions.

Each defendant claimed he was without funds, and required the assistance of free legal counsel. The Office of the Public Defender could only represent one of the accused, since potential conflicts of interest precluded that office from serving the needs of all seven individuals. The court was constrained to appoint six other independent counsel. I received notice of my appointment just two weeks after the robbery. I was assigned to represent Manuel Rosa Bandias, the pedestrian eventually arrested in New Jersey.

Back in the 1970s, courthouse and jail security had not yet reached today's level of sophistication. There were no video cameras, no X-ray or metal detectors, and no electronic automated cell doors. Lawyers were permitted to enter into the interior prison area, and meet with inmates in their cells. Today, visitors to the lock-up venture no further than the consultation room at the front reception area.

I first met Bandias in cell block D where he was still undergoing isolation. He claimed to speak no English, so I asked a passing guard if he might locate another inmate to serve as interpreter. Soon I was joined in cell #213, an 8' x12' box, by Enrico, who was doing three to 16 months for drug possession. The guard slammed the iron door behind us, as an ever escalating sense of claustrophobia swept over my body. The two prisoners began to speak in Spanish.

"He say he not guilty of no robbery, man. He don't even know these six other guys the cops arrested," Enrico explained. The men again spoke back and forth in their native tongue.

"He was in New Jersey trying to find work. He was

never in Pennsylvania," Enrico assured me.

I believed my client. I had to. That was my job. Had I not believed him, I could not have effectively represented him, a breach of my duty to the court to energetically defend the accused. I began to diligently prepare for trial, which was scheduled to occur in just three short months.

- - - - - - - - - - -

"All rise," the tipstaff announced, as Judge Griffith ascended the bench. Courtroom No. 1 was larger in area than any other two courtrooms combined. But with seven defendants, seven defense counsel, two assistant district attorneys, and three police prosecutors, there was a need to place several separate expansive counsel tables in the well of the courtroom. Nineteen participants faced both His Honor and the Ten Commandments reposing upon the wall to the left of the judge. I started to read the familiar plaque. My eyes fell upon one particular sentence: *Thou shall not bear false witness.*

"Is the Commonwealth prepared to proceed?" Judge Griffith inquired. And so began the four day trial. Matthew, the young victim, testified that he had briefly glanced at each of the robbers before he was dragged into the walk-in cooler. He thought he recognized all of the defendants, but he couldn't be positive. Grandmother Russo did not appear as a witness. Her health had declined dramatically and her doctors believed the strain of a trial might overwhelm her.

Frank, the bartender, was the strongest Commonwealth witness. He recognized all seven defendants, including my client, Manuel Rosa Bandias. My cross-examination did not dissuade him from this observation.

My patient friends, the courtroom benches, maintained their silent vigil over the proceedings. They were occupied by scores of family members and friends of both the defendants and the victims. Lookout's cousin,

Serena, who took the bus each day from Queens, New York, sat next to Mrs. Russo's next door neighbor. Guzman's mother shared a seat with Matthew's best friend, Eddie. Each spectator neither understood nor questioned the relationship of the person who was randomly located to the immediate left or right. I turned around to gaze at the multitude of concerned, quizzical, and anxious faces. Few courthouse observers could recall when last Courtroom No. 1 had been filled to capacity.

On the morning of the third day of trial, the court-appointed interpreter turned toward me and whispered in my ear.

"Bandias says he wants to take the witness stand."

This surprised me, since the other six defendants had wisely declined to be heard, a judicious exercise of their constitutional right not to incriminate themselves. I suggested that Bandias reconsider, since I now believed, as a result of the trial testimony, that he was guilty. It had become clear to me during the course of the proceedings that my client had lied to me regarding every major detail of the case. It was obvious, as an example, from his interaction with the other defendants during recesses in the trial, that he maintained a long and colorful friendship with his co-conspirators. This was apparent as the seven defendants sat huddled together in the prison "bull pen" area next to the courtroom, outside the earshot of the jury and spectators. One of the guards, who spoke Spanish, quietly confided to me that these bandits, during court recesses, often discussed their exploits, spanning a history of several years. I confronted Bandias with my suspicions, during the luncheon break.

"You told me you didn't know the other six defendants, and that you had independently traveled to New Jersey to seek work."

"Si," Bandias responded without hesitation as I sat in his cramped cell with Enrico, the informal jailhouse interpreter.

"That's a lie," I snapped. "The guards overheard you

bragging about previous crimes you pulled off with the other defendants. Everything you've told me has proven to be untrue. I won't assist you in court if you attempt to introduce perjured testimony."

Bandias was noticeably shaken, and the sneer began to disappear from his face.

"I won't need your help," the seasoned veteran of the judicial system advised the interpreter and me as he quickly recovered. "I'll handle the jury without you."

Trial resumed promptly at 1:30 p.m. I asked to approach the bench, outside the hearing of the jury. Bandias stood by my side.

"Your Honor," I began, "my client wishes to take the witness stand in his own defense. I'm inclined to believe he will submit perjured testimony. I refuse to assist in the presentation of same. Mr. Bandias has chosen to pursue his testimony without the assistance of counsel."

"I don't want a lawyer," my client advised the court through the interpreter. "I want to tell the jury my side of the story."

Judge Griffith pondered for a judicial moment. "Very well, Mr. Fox, the court acknowledges your dilemma. You are excused from assisting the defendant with regard to his direct examination, but in all other particulars, you shall remain his attorney of record."

Confident Bandias strode to the witness box. The interpreter told him to raise his right hand, so that the oath might be administered.

"Do you swear before Almighty God, the Searcher of all hearts, that the testimony you are about to give, shall be the Truth, the whole Truth, and nothing but the Truth, so as you shall answer unto God on the last great day?"

The formal court-appointed interpreter translated the court clerk's inquiry, as she looked into the defendant's dark, piercing eyes.

"Si," Bandias responded. Then he took the witness seat positioned immediately below the Ten Commandments.

Bandias turned to the jury, and stated unequivocally

that he was an innocent man unjustly accused. He assured the 12 citizens chosen to hear this case that he did not know the other six defendants, and on the night in question, he was searching alone for work in New Jersey.

The assistant district attorney's cross-examination failed to discredit the defendant. The prosecutor was unaware that a prison guard seated in the bull pen could have refuted the defendant's testimony, and the prison guard, who had not observed the trial, was unaware that his testimony might have been of value in proving that all the defendants knew each other. I could not ethically advise the court or the district attorney of the guard's potentially damaging testimony, for I had been retained to assist the defendant.

The assistant district attorney struggled onward with the questioning of the treacherous Bandias.

"Were you not present in court when the bartender positively identified you as being in Bethlehem with the other defendants on the night of this vicious robbery?"

"Si," Bandias confirmed through the interpreter, "but perhaps the bartender mistook me for someone else. I am often mistaken for someone else."

"Who might that be?" the prosecutor asked.

The defendant pointed into the midst of the benches - toward the seventh or eighth row of the spectators' area. Slowly a man stood up. The courtroom grew silent as the significance of this orchestrated moment became clear. I looked carefully at the stranger, and then returned my gaze to the defendant seated in the witness box. The jury engaged in the same comparison, and probably reached the same conclusion I did: The defendant had a brother - an identical twin. The seeds of reasonable doubt had been planted.

- - - - - - - - - - - -

"Have you reached a verdict?" the judge asked the jury after its return from its six-hour deliberation.

"We have," the forelady responded.

Packo, Ringleader, Lookout, Shotgun, Angel, and

Guzman were found guilty of all charges. Bandias was acquitted, and walked out of Courtroom No. 1 a free man. His twin brother drove him back to Brooklyn for a victory dinner with family and friends. I was not invited to this celebration.

The six convicted co-defendants were remanded to the custody of the Northampton County Prison, to await sentencing. Because of the severity of their crimes, I expected that each felon would receive a minimum 10-year sentence of incarceration.

It had been two weeks since conclusion of the trial. I had been assigned my next case, and had obtained access into the Northampton County Prison to talk with yet another indigent client. As I proceeded on the first floor through the general prison population toward cell block A, I heard a voice summon me.

"Hey! Abogado!"

I looked up toward the second floor tier of cells. Three men were leaning over the iron railing, waving at me. They looked vaguely familiar. Yes, there stood Packo, Lookout, and Guzman, the latter of whom appeared to have just awakened from a pleasant morning nap.

"Hey, Abogado," Packo repeated. "You do good job for Bandias. He get off scot-free!"

I hesitated to engage in this impromptu conversation. It would not have been the first time some inmate spit on me from one of the higher elevations. Moreover, I was not inclined to accept accolades for an acquittal predicated upon perjured testimony.

"It no matter, though. Bandias dead now!" Packo announced in a detached, almost disinterested manner.

"Dead?" I yelled above the never-ending jailhouse clamor.

"Si. He and his twin brother. They try to rob a liquor store back home. Got their heads blown off."

The three men slowly turned away and entered an awaiting cell. An important card game had already begun without them.

That afternoon, I called the Brooklyn District Attorney's office, and inquired if there had been a recent attempted robbery of a liquor store involving one Manuel Rosa Bandias. That office sent me the police report. A week earlier two men had entered a liquor store just before it was scheduled to close. They were about to pistol-whip the night clerk when the owner appeared from the back room brandishing a shotgun. Both criminals were decapitated by the ensuing blasts.

CHAPTER TWENTY-FOUR:
THE AGED PRACTITIONER

One of the ironies of practicing law is that the older a lawyer becomes, the greater is his or her ability to earn a living. Not so with other gladiators or paid gunslingers. Quarterbacks generally lose their touch by age 40. Professional wrestlers before that. But an aged attorney can go 10 rounds in court, charging more than a young practitioner, predicated solely upon his perceived vast years of experience. The sweetest music comes from the oldest violins, the most aromatic wines from properly seasoned vats.

The same rule applies to jurists. To be a good judge, one needs two attributes that naturally come with time: gray hair to look distinguished; and hemorrhoids to appear concerned. I smiled in the mirror when my first strands of silver hair made their debut. I immediately raised my hourly billing rate by $25. Not one client objected, even though I hadn't grown any wiser. It didn't matter, however, for I now appeared to be more intelligent, and similar to other forms of magic, it was the illusion that sufficed.

"It's time you start wearing bifocals," my optometrist announced just after I turned 40. "Now we have the new type of glasses that hide the fact that you're wearing them. No one will ever know."

"I want the type of old-fashioned spectacles my grandfather used to wear," I announced. "I hope to look as old as possible." The optometrist complied. I raised my hourly billing rate another $25. No one objected.

Now that I've seen my 50th birthday come and go, more often than not I find that the attorney representing the other litigant across the table is younger than I am. Some are just kids, who weren't even born when I first began to practice law. They come from a different world, and as a result, their perception of things both pertaining to the litigation and to the world in general differs vastly from my aged viewpoint. These young lawyers carry little computers in the palm of their hands, and talk with their 4-year-old children via cell phones. These fledgling bucks look upon me as if I were a dinosaur, a dying breed of mouthpiece whose bifocals and gray hair signal that one of my feet is already in the grave. They figure that if an appeal is filed on behalf of their clients, I probably won't live long enough to draft a responsive brief.

I am old, and more surprised than anyone else that I've made it this far. When I look back, I can't believe how significantly things have changed in such a relatively short period of time. It's been a good life, but I don't want to be 25 again. I paid to see the show once, and I got my money's worth. Now that it's nearing time to leave, I'm prepared to go without regret. Quite frankly, life before fax machines appealed to me. I'm hopeful that my next stop doesn't have any.

I'm so old, I can remember when, as children, we played outside in all types of weather, because there were no televisions, or other glowing screens to steal away our youth or our imagination. Then came the first television sets the size of refrigerators, possessing six-inch black and white screens. We stared transfixed as fuzzy images danced on three separate channels before our astonished eyes.

Nowadays, kids have access to everything. As a result, they have nothing. I watch as young parents struggle to keep their offspring "occupied" and "amused" every waking minute. I don't recall that my parents labored with such a burden. We played with marbles, or the container in which the marbles came.

It was television that began to change the world - and

not necessarily for the better. It affected all of us, insidiously, for no one realized at the time the degree to which it began to transform our thinking. I would come home from grade school and watch *Ozzie and Harriet* and *Leave it to Beaver*. Each of these shows, and there were others - *The Donna Reed Show* and *Father Knows Best*, just to name a few, depicted white nuclear families whose biggest confrontational issues evolved over what cereal should be eaten at breakfast, or who the lucky girl was that Wally would eventually take to the prom. The all-knowing husband worked, the wife smiled and kept the house immaculate, and the siblings rarely fought. Never was an ill word spoken in anger by anyone.

I, on the other hand, was obviously the only person in the world to live in a dysfunctional family. My mother rarely cooked dinner. After working outside the home all day, she would drive her battered Morris Minor car (the English equivalent of the VW Bug) home, boil some frozen hot dogs, and throw them on a plate. When my father arrived after his hard day, he would sit silently in the living room, reading the newspaper. The only thing my parents had in common was children, none of whom was going to the prom. I'm not complaining. As I look back now, I realize things weren't so bad. We never starved, Mom and Dad both had jobs, paid the bills, never got drunk or took drugs, kept a roof over our heads, and in their own strange ways, loved us. But Dad wasn't Ozzie, and Mom wasn't Harriet, or Donna Reed, or June Cleaver. She was just tired.

The bastards who concocted those stinking television programs should have been obligated, similar to tobacco companies, to place warning labels on their dangerous products:

WARNING

The show you are about to watch depicts
families that do not exist, engaging
in artificial and superficially contrived

pleasantries unknown to anyone other
than those individuals laboring in the
abnormal atmosphere of a Hollywood
television production company. Parental
discretion should be exercised regarding
viewing by children under the age of 12,
since repeated viewing will cause the
impressionable, undeveloped adolescent
mind to conclude that something is terribly
wrong with the adolescent's lot in life,
parents, siblings or environment.
More productive and beneficial time can
and should be spent playing marbles.

I'm so old, I now look back in disbelief at what was once thought to be entertaining. Physical and mental challenges were considered fair game for ridicule. Porky Pig stuttered; Daffy Duck exhibited a speech impediment lisp. Mortimer Snerd, the dummy utilized on nation-wide television by ventriloquist Edgar Bergen was depicted as being humorous, merely because he was a low IQ idiot. On the other hand, I'm so old I can also remember when television exhibited some common sense. Back when I was a kid, there was no depiction of violence. Murder took place off-camera. No cowboy ever shot anyone. Once in a while Roy Rogers, the Lone Ranger, or Gene Autry would shoot a gun out of some bad guy's hand, but blood never flowed. I'm so old I can remember when juveniles didn't bludgeon each other or anyone else. If a child is subjected to a continuous stream of bloodshed, who among us should be surprised today that the courts are filled with the end product of such mayhem? He who troubleth his own house shall inherit the wind.

I'm so old I can remember when a penny could actually be used to buy something, including candy, or 12 minutes on a parking meter. A letter could be sent anywhere with just a three cent stamp. Five & 10 cent stores were exactly that. If I had been good, Mom would give me a nickel and a dime, and let me go shopping for neat things like baby turtles - and marbles. The hardwood floors at the 5 & 10 creaked even under my modest weight. People sat nearby at the soda fountain sipping five cent cokes, trying to cool off, because there was no air conditioning. People knew their neighbors back then, since everyone sat on their porches for a breath of night air. As a result, we could go trick-or-treating on Halloween in our neighborhood without the fear of being poisoned.

Our lives were not encumbered or threatened by an unseen enemy. Travelers walked from airport terminals into waiting airplanes, unaccompanied by hijackers or their bombs. There were no machines required to scan our luggage or us. There was a time in the distant past when I could walk into any courthouse, using any door originally designed by the architect. Now I'm filmed, searched, and documented at the one guarded entranceway.

I can remember when telephones were first produced in a color other than black, and when you could walk on the beach without listening to another vacationer's one-sided cell phone conversation. I stared in awe the first day I saw someone carrying a transistor A.M. radio. It wasn't plugged into an electrical outlet. The Polaroid camera was the eighth wonder of the world - black and white pictures developed before my eyes in just five minutes. There were no skateboards, compact discs, or contact lenses. No pierced navels, and only those in the naval service sported tattoos. Women didn't wrestle on television. American Indians lived on reservations, and gambling was considered a crime. Now, the masses frequent the reservations to gamble, and the Indians are the pit bosses.

There was a time when the same type of diaper was used for both boy and girl babies. Trolleys ran on trolley tracks without expending a drop of gasoline. We wrapped our sandwiches with wax paper, rather than sealing them in petroleum products. Cash registers registered cash. No astronaut's dune-buggy was left behind to defile the surface of the moon. Milk and eggs were delivered door to door.

Motorcyclists didn't wear helmets. There was no Federal Express, but things got there anyway. "Instant gratification" was not a phrase applicable to the long distance purchase of retail goods. There were no malls - just local merchants giving out green stamps. After I had saved 88 books, I redeemed them for a BB gun.

There was no Alzheimers disease, because people weren't forced to live so long. There was no AIDS or organ transplants, but there was Polio and children lying in iron lung machines. They lined us up in third grade to receive Polio shots, administered by unfriendly nurses who utilized needles attached to glass syringes. Some guy named Dr. Salk had found a cure. We would all be saved. Doctors could be trusted, because they cared enough to make house calls, and they weren't controlled by the insurance industry. As a result, medical malpractice lawsuits were unheard of. No one sued the kind doctor who knew your grandparents, and accepted payment on the installment plan.

I look across the conference table at the 26-year-old attorney representing his client. This hatchling from law school was never subject to the draft, and thinks of Vietnam as an exotic vacation spot. I can't ask him where he was when Kennedy was shot. He has only owned cars that have come equipped with seat belts.

I'm not suggesting that the world has gone mad, or that once upon a time it might have been a better place. Rather, I've grown old, and I'm glad.